To my two oldest children, **Angel** and **Tony**. Thank you for inspiring me to write this book and helping me see the software development learning process through the eyes of bright young teens.

And to my other four wonderful children. Thank you for the countless hours of joyful distractions.

www.mascotbooks.com

Code for Teens: The Awesome Beginner's Guide to Programming

For more information, please contact:
Mascot Books
620 Herndon Parkway #320
Herndon, VA 20170
info@mascotbooks.com

Library of Congress Control Number: 2018902079

CPSIA Code: PRTWP0218A
ISBN-13: 978-1-68401-960-1

Printed in Malaysia

Code
for Teens

The Awesome Beginner's Guide to Programming

Written by
Jeremy Moritz

Illustrated by
Christine Moritz

Volume 1: JavaScript

Table of Contents

Foreword

By *Sarah Phelps, Computer Science Educator*

When Jeremy first asked me about writing the foreword for his book, I was excited and incredibly honored. Now, you should know that I am not a programmer. What I bring to this conversation is knowledge of children. I have been an elementary teacher for ten years now, and I developed a program for my school district with a goal to introduce kids to computer science and build an interest in pursuing it as they continue through school. I have done a ton of research, attended technology education conferences and trainings, and frequently consult with my personal software engineer: my husband. My experience in teaching and understanding how kids learn has helped me find resources and tools that are engaging and successful at teaching the fundamentals of computer science, so I began sharing these resources in technology conferences and children's STEM workshops around the country.

At one such conference and workshop, I met Jeremy and Christine and their many children. From the oldest to the youngest, the Moritz kids are full of enthusiasm for coding and learning in general. Their parents have inspired a desire to learn about the world around them in a way I only hope I am continually imparting to the students I teach.

Jeremy and I bonded in our belief that teaching kids programming is powerful. As he says in this book, being able to program a computer is like a superpower. The skills acquired in learning how to code go beyond just computer science, however. Computational thinking builds problem solving and logic skills that can be applied to nearly any subject. It gives kids an outlet to create and pushes them to think outside the box. Beyond that, programming prepares them to thrive in a global market. These are the skills for which employers will be searching.

Code for Teens is the perfect tool to help children and young teenagers learn JavaScript, the most commonly used programming language in software engineering. This book is entertaining and keeps the reader engaged. The text is well organized and has a great balance of directed practice and independent exploration with easy-to-follow exercises. Furthermore, Christine's amazing drawings are eye-catching and clever!

But, most important of all, the book empowers children to teach themselves, which is actually something I believe to be missing from much of the education our children receive. Educators are often telling kids to wait—as though they could not possibly understand something so impressive without the help of a "smart" adult. This book proves to them that they can do just that—move at their own pace and figure things out on their own.

The chapter quizzes provide a check-in for kids to test their knowledge. And don't worry: all the answers are in the back if, like me, you wouldn't know where to begin in helping. That being said, why not work alongside your child? As I was reviewing the text, I couldn't help opening up my own tab and trying it out myself.

Code for Teens is an excellent resource for any classroom, homeschool library, or a gift for that inquisitive youngster who is ready to take on a new challenge. What a remarkable feeling to discover one's ability to change the world! I cannot wait to share this book with the students I teach, and even more so with my own children, who I hope continue to develop and maintain a positive "learnitude" (as Jeremy calls it) throughout their lives!

Introduction

Why Learn to Code?

Starting with Chapter 1, every page of this book is in here with the goal of teaching you how to read and write computer code. Hundreds of pages and drills and dozens of projects and games are dedicated to this purpose. Before you get much further, this might be a great time to ask yourself an important question: Why should I even learn to code?

Well the long answer probably involves something about coding—also called "software engineering"—being one of the fastest growing industries in the world. There ought to be some comparison about this being a modern-day equivalent to the value of learning a skilled trade in past generations. Perhaps it should be mentioned that programmers are in extremely high demand, and this leads to excellent pay, comfortable work environments, flexible hours, greater job satisfaction, long-term career security, blah, blah, blah...

But really...the answer is simple:

Superpowers.

Harry Potter was whisked away to Hogwarts to hone his wizardry skills. Gifted youngsters attended Professor X's school to master their mutant abilities. And you, dear reader, will take control of the most valuable superpower in the natural world: programmable code.

Have you ever had a great idea about what some company or person should invent someday? Have you ever been asked to do some boring, repetitive task that you knew would take a loooong time and you wished there were some machine that could just do all that work for you? Have you seen the way some game works and thought, "Yeah, it's good, but it would sure be a lot better if only…"?

When good ideas like these occur, most poor muggles have no choice but to just sigh and let them float away. Such mysterious things are not for mere mortals, right? Well, by the end of this book, you will come to learn that you are more powerful than you know. You are designed with a remarkable brain capable of harnessing the great superpower of talking to machines and making them obey your commands.

By learning to code, you will open up a world of possibilities. You will be able to take the magical ideas in your head and turn some of them—the best ones— into reality.

Where to Start?

Once you've decided to learn how to program, you will soon find that you have a whole heapin' ton of options in front of you.

Learning to code is kinda like learning a new language. If you wanted to learn how to speak a second language, you might first ask yourself which language would be the most useful. Do your grandparents speak Chinese? Do you have an aunt from Japan or close friends who speak French in their home? Any of these factors might give you good insight on which language you'd most like to learn. But if you live in the U.S.A., you might choose to learn Spanish for the simple reason that it is much more commonly used than all other languages in the country combined (except English of course).

In a similar way to spoken languages, there are dozens of marvelous programming languages that you can learn—including Java, Python, C#, PHP, Go, C++ and more—but there is one programming language that definitely tops the list:

JavaScript!

JavaScript is the most common programming language of them all and is used in over 90% of all websites! JavaScript makes websites move and respond to what a user touches and types. And it's also a useful tool for games and mobile apps! With more and more businesses going online and people browsing on their phones, JavaScript is becoming more valuable every year.

So can you guess which programming language you will learn in this book?!

Wow! You guessed it! JavaScript!! (Gosh, you're good…I think I'll need to make the questions harder next time...)

Maximatize Your Learnitude and Funhavingness!

When I wrote that header, I honestly thought I was making up the word "learnitude"... turns out it's a real word! It means "the attitude of learning". That actually works well, doesn't it? And I just learned something new myself. Awesome!

Anyway, where was I going with this?...Oh yeah!

This book is designed for you to teach yourself how to code without your parents' or teachers' help. Because let's face it: most of them probably don't know anything about how to code anyway. And if they do, they're probably so busy saving the world with their superpowers that they don't have time to walk you through everything step-by-step.

Well fear not, dear reader! This book moves at YOUR pace. Every chapter includes a review section and lots of drills. If you don't understand something right away, you should be able to get it by the end of the chapter review, and the coding drills will help it stay planted firmly in your brain for the future. For some readers, this book may contain more review and more drills than you need. If that's you, then I recommend you still glance over each of them and be sure you can mentally figure out the answer even if you don't write it down. Be honest with yourself about what will help you the best.

Try typing the code along with the book and sometimes try making small changes to see if the code functions a little differently.

The concepts you'll learn in this book build on each other, so do your best to really understand each topic before moving to later chapters. There's also a glossary in the back if you see a word and you've forgotten what it means (that's just brain hiccups—happens to all of us).

Another piece of good news: if you are ever stuck on a problem, ALL of the answers are in the back of the book. It's like having the Teacher's Guide built right in! Though you should know that sometimes there could be more than one right answer. Definitely try to understand how to do it the way the book teaches, but don't sweat it if your version is a little different and still works.

Lastly, programming should be fun! Maybe not all the time, but overall, it should feel a lot like solving puzzles or working through a thinking game. Don't get too down on yourself if you're struggling through a concept. Try your best to figure it out, but don't stall on something if you feel you're not making progress. Check the answers in the back, then just move on and come back to the topic later. It's all part of the adventure.

Now let's remove the gloves and learn to use your special new abilities!

A Word for Parents

Top Secret: No Kids Allowed!

The next couple pages contain a message to the *parents*! Kids, if you see this confidential, highly classified, top secret, Level 5 clearance section, now is the time to fulfill your contractual obligation to hand the book to your folks…and get it back two pages later.

Parents, if you made the brilliant decision to buy this book for your child or teenager, I'm going to assume you probably have some understanding of how beneficial it is for him/her to learn how to code. Software engineering (a.k.a. "coding") is one of the most in-demand, high-paying careers in the world right now, and it's becoming even more valuable every year. By learning to code, your child is developing his/her mind in practical ways, and taking an important step toward building skills that could remain relevant throughout his/her adult life.

But knowing something is valuable and actually knowing what to do about it are two very different things! Maybe you've never written a line of code in your life. Maybe you don't know a computer monitor from a hall monitor or a browser from a Schnauzer!

On the other hand, maybe you're an engineering professional, and you want your kids to enjoy the same career freedom and security that you experience every day. But who has the time and patience and know-how to teach what you've learned? Teaching certainly requires a different set of skills than simply knowing how to do the work.

Either way, this book is for YOU…to give to your kids and make them read it.

When I set out to write this book, my goal was to create a text that children and teenagers (really, anyone with at least a 6th grade reading level) could use to teach themselves to code without requiring input from knowledgeable parents or teachers.

As an involved, homeschooling father of six, I have gained much practical insight into how children learn. From my experience, it is very difficult to find teaching materials that will teach a real multi-purpose coding language consistently at a child's pace. My own children have often showed me the work

they've done from other resources without being able to explain their own code, much less build any of it from scratch without copying from a book. The desire to correct this for my own kids was the initial inspiration for this book.

When learning to code, children tend to benefit from more repetition, review, and drilling than adults need. They often require less lecturing and more hands-on work intermixed within the lessons. Knowledge and skills may be quickly forgotten if not coupled with frequent opportunities to use them in practical lessons and activities.

I think you'll find that this book is well suited to the pace at which your child or teen learns naturally. Beyond that, it is filled with colorful, original illustrations (designed by my talented wife Christine) and infused with humor—okay…"Dad jokes"—on almost every page to help encourage the reader's attention and enjoyment.

Now, even though the book is intended to make it possible for children to learn without any help, I must acknowledge that it will be even better if you, the parent who loves them, are available to provide a small degree of accountability. I want to emphasize something strongly though: you do NOT need to know ANYTHING about coding! Early in the training, your child will be expected to create and save a document (we call it the "Workbook") to keep his/her own answers to the quizzes and drills. All of the correct answers are in the back of the book, so it's possible for the child to check his/her own work without help.

However—and this may alarm you—sometimes when kids are given the opportunity to check all their own work with no oversight, they don't follow through to actually doing all of the assigned work. Hopefully, you were sitting down when you read that. ;-) Seriously though, if you are checking your child's answers against the key, this additional accountability will likely help him/her to take the work more seriously and be more diligent about completing it all.

Another thing that will provide a huge benefit to your child's learning process: ask to see his/her work. You don't have to even try to understand it; just let your child explain it to you. And when you see the work, show a little enthusiasm! You don't need to know one thing about coding in order to feign some excitement about it.

Last thing: Please read the short Introduction that precedes this section. You will get a clearer picture of the nature of this book and how your child may get the most out of it.

I'm excited that your child or teenager has taken this huge first step in learning the extremely useful and relevant skill of coding. I hope you find this book to be a valuable resource to start the journey!

1 HELLO WORLD!

Are you ready to write your first line of **code**? We just need to assemble a few materials, and we'll get right to it. Let's do this!

Computer, Browser, and Console

The first thing you'll need is a **computer**—either a desktop, laptop, or Chromebook (NOT a smartphone or tablet!). If you don't have a computer with you, you can use one at the library or something. Or ask a friend. Or build one out of pipe cleaners, redstone, and hardened mash potatoes (...not recommended).

Your computer runs on an **operating system**: Windows (for PCs), MacOS (for Macs), ChromeOS (for Chromebooks), or Linux (for nerds). You should know which of these operating systems your computer uses.

Secondly, you'll need to have Google **Chrome** on this computer. Chrome is an **internet browser**—a program that people use to go to websites. You might already have this installed on your computer. The icon looks like a Poké Ball with four different colors.

By the way, did you notice how some of these words are in **bold**? That is how I indicate that this word is important and defined in the glossary at the back of the book. What's a **glossary** you ask? It's like a dictionary that only has terms from this book. Check it out in the back of the book now!

If you don't have Chrome on your computer, you can download it by opening up some other internet browser (Firefox, Safari, Edge, or IE), doing a Google search for "Download Chrome," then just following the directions in the first result.

Okay, now that you have Chrome on your computer, open it up, click into the address bar, type `about:blank`, and press **ENTER** (or **RETURN** if you're on a Mac). You should now see a blank screen. Note: the specific keys to type are also in **bold**, but they are CAPITALIZED too. These *don't* have definitions in the glossary...cuz they're just keys on your keyboard.

Now it's time to open the console! The **console** is part of Chrome's top-secret developer tools. Now that you're becoming a JavaScript developer, you get to use it too! Simply hold down the **CTRL** and **SHIFT** keys (or the **COMMAND** and **OPTION** keys if you're on a Mac) and press the J key. Note: For future reference, key combinations like this one will be shown this way "**CTRL+SHIFT+J** (or **COMMAND+OPTION+J** on a Mac)".

After you press those keys, you should see a new lower section of the screen that has an angle bracket in the upper left part of it. If you *don't* see this area when you use the **CTRL+SHIFT+J** (or **COMMAND+OPTION+J** on a Mac) shortcut, you may also get to it by right-clicking on any empty area of the page and selecting "Inspect" from the dropdown menu, then selecting the "Console" tab as shown in the illustration.

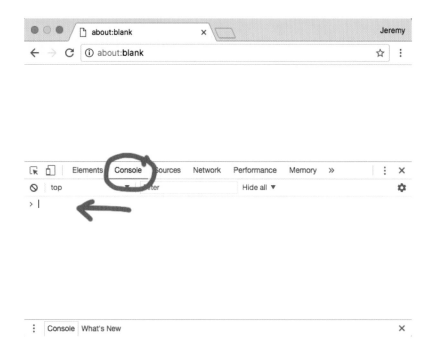

As a side note, if you move your cursor over the light gray bar until you get a double-arrow symbol, you should be able to click and drag this box up to make it as large as possible. Definitely do this to give yourself more room to type.

Now that you've expanded that box a bit, click right next to the angle bracket. You should get a blinking cursor and be able to type some text. Here is your first line of code. Type this (including the quotes) and pay special attention to the semicolon key ; (near the middle-right of your keyboard) as this will be used many times at the end of code statements:

```
"Hello World!";
```

Then press **ENTER** (or **RETURN** on a Mac). You should see a response from the console with the words `"Hello World!"` repeated back to you. Notice, by the way, that the code you are expected to type is `colored with blue text` while the console responses are `colored in red`. This should make it easier to see what to type into the console. You'll later see examples of `code with black type`; this is just meant for you to read (not type yourself).

Now try this: press the **UP_ARROW** key on the keyboard. You can see the `"Hello World"`; text on the line again. Move the cursor to the front of that line and change it so it reads:

```
var greeting = "Hello World!";
```

Then press **ENTER** (if you're on a Mac, just remember from now on that **ENTER** always refers to the **RETURN** key). The response you should get back from the console is `undefined`. So far so good! Now type:

```
greeting;
```

and press **ENTER**. If you have done everything right so far, the console should return with the message `"Hello World!"`. And now, my friends, you can forever say that you've written and executed a teensy-tiny bit of **JavaScript**!

Follow the Leader

So…what's the point? What did we even do? THIS is coding?! I mean, who even cares if—

Whoa! Slow down there! I'm glad you asked. Really, I am! Believe me, I'm itching to explain it all to you soon, but first I'd like us to do a little trust exercise. Just follow along like a game of Simon Says or Follow the Leader. Type everything I show here (only the `blue text with gray highlights`) into the console. End each line by pressing the **ENTER** key, and make sure you're getting the expected responses. Type this:

```
5 + 8;
```
Console should respond with: `13`

```
7 - 3 + 6;
```
Response: `10`

Type (notice this one uses the * which is the *multiplied by* symbol in coding):
```
var x = 3; 4 * x;
```
Response: `12`

```
x + x;
```
Response: `6`

Notice on that last one the value of x carried over from previous statements.
Now try this:
```
x = 200;
```

This is assigning a *new* value to x. Now press **UP_ARROW** two times until you see this again:
```
x + x;
```

After pressing **ENTER**, you'll see that the response is now `400` because the value of x has changed. Okay just a few more, then I'll explain what these are about.

Type (notice this one uses the / which is the *divided by* symbol in coding):
```
x / 100;
```
Response: `2`

```
(x - 50) / 5;
```
Response: `30`

```
(x - 50) / (5 - 1);
```
Response: `37.5`

```
"I hope I grow to be " + x + " years old!";
```
Response: `"I hope I grow to be 200 years old!"`

```
"Hmm... maybe " + (x / 2) + " is old enough.";
```
Response: `"Hmm... maybe 100 is old enough."`

How was that? Were there any of these lines that surprised you? I haven't explained any of them yet, but I'll bet you picked up on a few things already, right?

Did you make any mistakes along the way? I hope so. JavaScript **engineers** make mistakes almost every single day. A major part of being a good **programmer** is learning how to identify our mistakes (called "**bugs**") and fix them (**i.e.**, squash them). We'll talk more about that in this chapter and future chapters too. But first, let's talk about what each of the pieces of your JavaScript code means and how each is interpreted (read) by the computer.

Syntax

JavaScript—like every other **programming language**—follows a strict **syntax**. Syntax is like the spelling and grammar of the language. Computers are not as smart as people. They can't figure out the general idea of what you mean the way a person can. Instead, the computer can only understand what you want to tell it if you type it in exactly the way that the computer expects to see it. The expected form is called the syntax.

We're about to type more stuff in the console, but do this one favor for me, real quick. Even if you still have your browser open from before, I'd like to start over to make sure we can easily get back to a screen like this again. So close down Chrome, then open it up again. Type in the address bar `about:blank` again, then use **CONTROL+SHIFT+J** (**COMMAND+OPTION+J** on a Mac) to open the console (by the way, you should definitely memorize that keyboard shortcut; you'll use it a lot!). The console should be clear again and ready for you to type commands.

Here are some examples of proper JavaScript syntax. Type each of these blue text statements in the console (be sure to type each line EXACTLY as written), and press **ENTER** after each one. Type:

```
var greetingFirstPart = "Hello";
```

Explanation: This is known as a JavaScript **statement**. Statements usually end with a semicolon (`;`). The keyword var at the beginning tells the computer (well, technically, it's not the *computer*, but the browser's JavaScript **interpreter**) that the next word `greetingFirstPart` will be a **variable**. Then the equals sign (`=`) tells the computer (err… *interpreter*) that we are *assigning* the value of `"Hello"` to the variable `greetingFirstPart` so it can be used later. Lots of big words in there, I know, but do try to learn them as we will be using them over and over and over. If you forget what they mean, remember that you can check the glossary in the back of the book for their definitions!

```
let greetingSecondPart = "World";
```
Console Response: `undefined`

Explanation: Another **assignment** statement. The keyword `let` does exactly the same thing as `var`. Okay, there are very slight differences, but explaining it would be unnecessarily confusing at this point, so don't worry about it yet. Just know that we will use `let` most of the time in this book, but you will still see `var` a lot in JavaScript code. In this assignment statement, we're assigning a **string** (`"World"`) to the new variable greetingSecondPart. The word `"World"` is known as a string because it's in quotes (we'll talk more about this in the next chapter). You might have also noticed that after you pressed **ENTER**, the console responded with `undefined`. That's nothing to be concerned about either. That simply means you have not told the JavaScript interpreter to **RETURN** (bring back) anything yet. It's like you told the interpreter "Write this down so we can use it later." The interpreter obeyed your command and is now patiently awaiting further instructions.

As a side note, if you find that you make a mistake while copying my code and you get unexpected errors that you don't understand, simply refresh the Chrome browser window (look for a "looping around" button near the top of the window) and try again. You'll learn other ways to deal with mistakes later, but no need to worry about those just yet. Now type:

```
let singleSpace = " ";
```
Response: `undefined`

Explanation: Statement assigning a string (containing a single space between the quotes) to a new variable called `singleSpace`. Notice also that *assignments always have exactly one variable on the left side of the equals sign*. For example, `let x = 2 + 2;` is valid JavaScript, but `2 + 2 = let x;` and `2 + 2 = x;` are both *not* valid.

```
let fullGreeting = greetingFirstPart + singleSpace + greetingSecondPart;
```
Response: `undefined`

Explanation: Yet another assignment statement. Did you notice, by the way, that the variable names—`greetingFirstPart`, `greetingSecondPart`, `singleSpace` and `fullGreeting`—have a capital letter in each of the inner words? And also no space between the inner words? That's on purpose. Variable names must never have a space in them. Also, they should ideally be in "camel case" (usually written as **camelCase**), which means that they should start with a lowercase letter, and use a single capital letter at the start of each word (or acronym) that is part of the variable. It's called camelCase because the capital letters in the middle of the word kinda look like the hump(s) on a camel's back. If this confuses you, keep reading. You'll see so many examples of camelCase variables that it will look very natural to you soon enough.

```
fullGreeting = fullGreeting + "!!";
```
Response: `undefined`

Explanation: In this assignment statement, we're adding an extra string (`"!!"`) to the end of `fullGreeting` and then assigning that new, longer string to the same variable called `fullGreeting`. Did you notice we're not using the keyword `let`? Why not? Because `let` indicates that we're creating (also called *declaring*) a new variable. In this case, we're not creating any new variables. The variable `fullGreeting` already exists so we're not going to use the `let` keyword anymore when we reference it.

```
fullGreeting;
```
Response: `"Hello World!!"`

Explanation: Now that we're not making another assignment, the computer (d'oh! *Interpreter!*) actually had something to RETURN (meaning, something to tell you)! It's like you ordered the interpreter, "Hey, go get the value of that variable from before and RETURN it to me!" So the response from the console was the actual value of the `fullGreeting` variable.

Simple Errors

Now that you know a bit of JavaScript syntax, let's make some syntax mistakes! As a programmer, syntax errors happen almost every day. The key is learning how to read the error messages you see, so you can quickly find and fix the syntax problems in your code.

Okay now I'd like you to open a new *tab* in chrome. Press **CONTROL+T** (**COMMAND+T** on a Mac). Type in the address bar `about:blank` again, then use the secret keyboard shortcut shared earlier to open the console (go back and find it again if you forgot it—memorize it this time!). The console should be clear again and ready for you to type commands. Type:

```
5 + ;
```
Response: `Uncaught SyntaxError: Unexpected token ;`

Now that response looks downright bizarre, doesn't it? Uncaught SyntaxError? Unexpected token? Whaaaaa?!

But look again…a little more closely this time. `Uncaught SyntaxError` just means there is something wrong with the syntax. In other words, what you wrote isn't actually a valid line of JavaScript. The interpreter—oops, I mean computer…No wait, interpreter IS what I meant! It's a *JavaScript interpreter*…Anyway, the interpreter can't read it and doesn't know what to do with it. `Unexpected token ;` means that the interpreter read something it didn't expect: in this case it was the semicolon (;).

So as the JavaScript interpreter was reading your line of code, it came to the semicolon, which signifies to the interpreter that we've reached the end of the statement. So the interpreter was all like, "That's it?! `5 + ;`? Huh?? 5 + WHAT?! That doesn't make any sense! That's not a complete statement! I didn't expect to see that `;` here, and now I'm all confused!"

The more you learn JavaScript, the more you'll come to appreciate these **error messages**. They're usually very helpful at pointing you to where you've made mistakes. Let's try making a few more mistakes. Type:

```
6 + 7);
```
Response: `Uncaught SyntaxError: Unexpected token )`

Explanation: You have a closing parenthesis ")" but no opening parenthesis! Parentheses (that's the plural form of parenthesis) always come in pairs. Also, they're usually called "parens" (pronounced "puh-RENZ") by JavaScript engineers. So if you ever have an opening paren ("puh-REN"), you need a closing paren too. And vice versa.

```
(1 + 2;)
```
Response: `Uncaught SyntaxError: Unexpected token ;`

Explanation: The semicolon `;` tells the JavaScript interpreter that it reached the end of the line BEFORE it got to the closing paren. That's why the ; was an `unexpected token`. Get it?

```
3 + newVariable;
```
Response: `Uncaught ReferenceError: newVariable is not defined`

Explanation: Now this error is not a SyntaxError but rather a ReferenceError. Can you tell what the problem is? Read the error message closely (that's what it's there for). It says: `newVariable is not defined`. There's your problem! You need to first **declare** the variable with something like this:

```
let newVariable = 24;
```
Response: `undefined`

Don't be concerned about the `undefined` response from the console. That's just because the console doesn't have anything to tell you right now. Next, press the **UP_ARROW** key two times until you get this statement again (then press **ENTER** to run the command):

```
3 + newVariable;
```
Response: `27`

Explanation: Now that the variable is *declared* and **defined** (i.e., it actually means something), the statement works just fine! What you did here is a simple example of **debugging**! You found an error in your code (a "bug"), and you squashed/fixed it! Let's squash one more bug, shall we?

```
let favoriteColor = "red";
```
Response: `undefined` // no problem yet (`undefined` just means "nothing to tell you")

```
let favoriteColor = "blue";
```
Response: `Uncaught SyntaxError: Identifier 'favoriteColor' has already been declared`

Explanation: Can you figure out this problem by reading the error message? The problem in this case is that we're using the `let` keyword for a variable that has already been declared once. The first time we used it, it was fine since `favoriteColor` was being declared for the first time. After that, we shouldn't use the `let` keyword again. The second statement will work just fine if we take it out, like so:

```
favoriteColor = "blue";
favoriteColor;
```
Response: `"blue"`

See how that works? By reading the error message and then trying the statement without the `let` keyword, we changed the value of the variable (and possibly even changed your favorite color!) from "`red`" to "`blue`".

As you may have guessed, we're only scratching the surface on the kinds of errors we will see when programming, but the important takeaway is this: don't be afraid of them. *The error messages are your friends.* Read those things! If you have trouble understanding them, try copying the error message and pasting it into a Google search. They will help you to quickly identify what you're doing wrong and fix it easily.

Follow Along: Average Meal Price Calculator

This is the first of the "Follow Along" projects you'll do in this book. These projects start off simple and will grow in complexity (and fun!) as you learn more about how to code.

Before going any further, please either close down Chrome and open it up again or just open a new tab and navigate to the all-blank

screen like you did before (this might seem like a pointless interruption, but the frequent repetition will help you remember all the steps tomorrow). Then open the console so it's ready when you want to type in your code.

Alright, with that out of the way, let's check out our first assignment!

We need to calculate the average price for a combo meal at Freckly Fred's Franks & Fries franchise (because ya know…we just need to, okay?!). Here's what we know:

Full Combo Menu:

Combo A - "Alpha Dog" (Hot Dog, Medium Fries, and a Drink) costs $6.75
Combo B - "Big Dog" (Hot Dog, Large Fries, and two Drinks) costs $7.50
Combo C - "Canine" (Hot Dog, 2 Small Fries, and a Dipping Sauce) costs $5.75
Combo D - "Double Dog" (Hot Dog, Large Fries, and a Smaller Hot Dog) costs $8

Now let's do this together and we'll show our work in the process. To start with, let's define what we want and what we don't want: do we care about the special combo names? Nope! Does it matter to us what's in each combo meal? Not really (though I personally think Combo C could maybe use an extra Dipping Sauce, but that's just me). So it looks like all we care about for this project is price. We're looking for the AVERAGE price of all these meals.

To get the average of any set of numbers, we must add the numbers together (to get the sum), then divide their sum by the number of items in the collection. For example, to get the average value of the two numbers 3 and 5, we would add them together to get the sum (8), then divide that sum by how many numbers there are (2 different numbers), giving us the average value of 4. In plain math, it would be: $(5 + 3) / 2 = 4$.

For the first code that we'll type, let's assign each of the values to a variable, which is almost always a good practice in JavaScript.

```
let comboAPrice = 6.75;
let comboBPrice = 7.5;
let comboCPrice = 5.75;
let comboDPrice = 8;
```

Now we have of all the prices individually for each combo. What's next? We need to add them together!

```
let sumOfComboPrices = comboAPrice + comboBPrice +
comboCPrice + comboDPrice;
```

Then divide that sum by the total number (the count) of combos that there are to get the average (remember that / means divided by)!

```
let numberOfCombos = 4;
let averagePrice = sumOfComboPrices / numberOfCombos;
```

Finally, let's print out the value to the console!

```
averagePrice;
```

Response: 7

So the average price for a combo meal at Freckly Fred's is $7.00! Great to know! Our boss will be so proud of us when we tell her tha—

Hey wait! This just in! It turns out Freckly Fred's has added a new combo!

Combo E - "E. Coli Dog" (2 Uncooked Hot Dogs, Small Fries and a Mystery Prize) costs $8.25

So let's make just a couple quick changes, and we'll get the new average:

```
let comboEPrice = 8.25;
sumOfComboPrices = sumOfComboPrices + comboEPrice;
```

Notice that we did NOT use `let` in the second assignment statement. That's because `sumOfComboPrices` has *already* been declared! We can't declare it a second time or we'll get an error. Instead, we'll change the existing value to be the sum that it was before PLUS the price of the new combo.

And let's update the number of combos too (notice, we are NOT using the let keyword because we're changing this existing variable, not declaring a new variable, remember?):

```
numberOfCombos = 5;
```

Now press **UP_ARROW** as many times as you need to until you see this line in the console again (don't press **ENTER** yet though!):

```
let averagePrice = sumOfComboPrices / numberOfCombos;
```

Now move your cursor to the front of the line (far left side) and delete the `let` keyword (since the variable already exists), so it should look like this (NOW you can press **ENTER**):

```
averagePrice = sumOfComboPrices / numberOfCombos;
```

Okay, now that we've made those changes, let's print out the new value!

```
averagePrice;
```

Response: `7.25`

Hooray! We have the final value, and now we know the NEW average price of a combo meal at Freckly Fred's Franks & Fries!

I hope you were able to follow along well with that little project. If not, I recommend you open a new tab in Chrome, open the console, and try the project one more time before moving on.

CHAPTER 1: QUIZ

Each chapter in this Section has a little quiz at the end. I recommend you take this whole quiz without looking back for any of the answers. This is meant to help you determine how well you retained the key concepts of this chapter.

Now pay special attention to this part: all of your answers need to be typed out and saved in a document you can use again and again. There are many ways to do this. If you or your parents have a Google account—or if you're willing to sign up for one (they're free)—I recommend opening a new tab in Chrome and going to http://docs.google.com to create a new document to keep all your quiz answers and review. This is something your parents will probably know how to do if you're unsure. If you don't have a Google account, you can use any word processor such as Microsoft Word, iWork Pages, or OpenOffice. If you prefer, you could even do this in a basic text editor like Notepad or TextEdit. But you should type out all of your answers to the Chapter Quizzes, Reviews, and Do It Yourself (DIY) Projects (and most of the Drills too). I'll refer to this document as your "**Workbook**."

One important hint: Remove the "smart quotes" option!

If you are creating the Workbook in Google docs: go to the "Tools" menu (at the top of the page), then click "Preferences…", then UNCHECK the boxes for "Automatically capitalize words" and "Use smart quotes."

If you're using Microsoft Word, OpenOffice, or Pages for your Workbook, you'll need to remove smart quotes a different way. Just do a Google search for "Turn off smart quotes in <name_of_your_program_here>" and follow the directions.

×

Preferences

☐ Automatically capitalize words
☐ Use smart quotes
✓ Automatically detect links

Trust me on this one. Get a parent to help you if you need, but don't skip this step. Your code will give you unexpected errors in later chapters if you don't do this!

There's one more thing I want you to keep in mind: *all* of the answers are in the back of the book. After you finish the quiz, you *must* check your answers to see if you missed anything. Even if you're pretty sure you got them all right, check them anyway. There are some questions that are intentionally tricky (so you need to check to be sure). If you're able to get a parent or another person to check your answers, that's even better!

Okay, I'll stop talking now. It's quiz time!

1. What URL address should you go to in order to get a completely empty page in Chrome?

2. What is the shortcut key combination to open the Chrome console?

3. What are the two keywords we've shown that may be used to declare a new variable?

4. What single character is usually found at the end of a statement?

5. What character means *divided by* when writing code?

6. What is the shortened form of the word "parenthesis"?

7. What kind of error would you get if you tried to run this statement?
    ```
    let sum = (9 + ; 3)
    ```

8. What kind of capitalization (i.e., casing) should you use with variable names in JavaScript?

9. Whenever you have an opening _____, you always need to also have a closing _____.

10. Is this valid JavaScript syntax? If not, why not?
    ```
    let myMood = "Curious about JavaScript";
    let myMood = "Excited to use my new superpowers";
    myMood;
    ```

11. What does a single equals sign imply in a statement?

CHAPTER 1: KEY CONCEPTS

Each chapter in this Section has this little breakdown of the key concepts. This is just meant to reference a few simple ideas from the chapter (in roughly the order they were introduced). Glance over this list and if there's anything you don't think you fully understand, look back in the chapter to review it so you can be sure you're ready to move on.
Okay now, here are the takeaways from this chapter:

- Required materials
- Opening blank page in new browser window or tab in Chrome
- Using the console in Chrome
- Variables
- Simple math operations
- JavaScript syntax
- camelCase
- Error messages

Whenever you get to a Drills section, you should type each line in the console. Don't hesitate to look in the back of the book if you'd like any help. Even if you already know how to do this, the drills will help you to continually remember these concepts going forward.

A. Try typing these valid code snippets in the console.

1.
```
let myFaveTopping = "pepperoni";
let my2ndFaveTopping = "sausage";
let ultimatePizza = myFaveTopping + " and " + my2ndFaveTopping;
ultimatePizza;
```

2.
```
var sumTotal = 6 + 7 + 8;
sumTotal;
```

3.
```
(8 * 3) / 6;
```

4.
```
var myBrotherAge = 11;
var mySisterAge = 13;
var numberOfSiblings = 2;
var mySiblingsAverageAge = (myBrotherAge + mySisterAge) / numberOfSiblings;
mySiblingsAverageAge;
```

5.
```
let coolMathValue = 5;
let coolMathAnswer = (20 / coolMathValue) + ((8 * coolMathValue) / (6 - 2));
coolMathAnswer;
```

6.
```
6 + " Foot " + 7 + " Foot";
```

7.
```
"Working " + 9 + " to " + 5;
```

8.
```
7 + "3"; // this one may surprise you!
```

9.
```
12 / 0; // this one may surprise you too!
```

B. What's wrong with each of these code snippets?

In this section, you're expected to determine what's wrong with each line. You will need to open your Workbook (the document you created yourself to store your answers) and write what you think is wrong with each line. Then check your answers with the back of the book (don't skip this step!). Hint: if you're not sure what's wrong with it, try typing some of these in the console to see if your good friends The Error Messages might show up to help!

1.
```
myUndeclaredVariable = 5;
```

2.
```
let famousQuote = "I like turtles;
```

3.
```
5 + 3 = x;
```

4.   `(4 * 7;)`

5.   `var somethingsBroken = 2 + (9 / (1 + 2);`

6.   `let somethingElseIsBroken = 4 + (5 - 2));`

7.   `12 + x = 15;`

8.   `let shouldntWeHaveASemicolon = "Yes we should"`

9.   `let notreallycamelcase = "Hard to read variable name";`

10.   `var ISTHISANYBETTER = "No, not really";`

11.   `let how_about_this = "Easier to read, but still not following convention";`

12.   `let IsThisCloseEnough = "So close, but not quite";`

13.   `let surely-this-counts-right = "Are you kidding? Those are minus signs!";`

14.   `let okayHowAboutThis = Good!`

Note: Be sure to read the Chapter 1 Drills Answers in the back of the book for some fun bonus info about the different casing examples in those snippets you just saw!

Do-It-Yourself (DIY): Average Age of Your Family

At the end of every chapter in the section, there is a special "Do It Yourself" project (also called a "DIY project") that utilizes concepts we've learned in the current chapter (and any previous chapters). You're welcome to do this project in the console. When you're done with it, highlight your code, copy it by pressing **CONTROL+C** (or **COMMAND+C** on a Mac), and then paste it into your Workbook by pressing **CONTROL+V** (or **COMMAND+V** on a Mac). Then compare your solution with the one at the end of the book. Ideally, you should do this after you're done, but it's okay to check it before you're done if you're struggling.

This DIY project is similar to the Follow Along project we did earlier. Here's your mission:

Determine the average age of all of the members in your immediate family (mom, dad, siblings, and you).

Close, then open Chrome, navigate to blank page, open the JavaScript console, and type all of your code in the console. Be sure to use variables (ideally with descriptive names like `ageOfBabyBrother`) for every number value.

If you ever get stuck trying to figure out any DIY project, consult the "Do It Yourself (DIY) Recommended Solution" in the back of the book.

2 TIME TO OPERATE

No matter what coding language you learn, you'll need to know a little something about **data types**. Every variable you set will have a certain data type to it, and the ability to identify it is a valuable part of coding. This will help you to avoid coding errors or to find and fix errors more quickly.

Numbers

Okay, let's start with an easy data type: **numbers**!

Numbers can be **positive** or **negative** (or 0 which is neither positive nor negative). They can have decimals or not, but numbers are never shown with quotes. Here are a few simple examples of numbers in JavaScript (don't forget to type blue text into the console! Check out the beginning of Chapter 1 if you've forgotten how to open up the Chrome console):

```
4
282038273
-38
51.9
0
-0.000087
```

Super simple, right? Let's move on!

Operations with Numbers

Common Operations

Doctor! These numbers! They won't make it on their own like this much longer. We need to OPERATE!

In Chapter 1, we played around a bit with these cool things called **operators**. We now get to bring them back and introduce a few new ones! Here's a quick review of operators:

Plus sign (+) is for *adding*: `4 + 4;`
Response: `8`

Minus sign (−) is for *subtracting*: `7 - 6;`
Response: `1`

Asterisk (*) is for *multiplying*: `3 * 4;`
Response: `12`

Forward slash (/) is for *dividing*: `15 / 5;`
Response: `3`

When we put them together in coding, we use parens—(and)—to separate out each segment and make things more readable. Type these statements in the console. Each one should give you a single-digit number as the response:

```
3 * (2 + 1);
(3 + 9) / (10 - 6);
(2 + (3 * 4)) / (6 + 1);
(2 * (5 - (8 / 2))) * (3 + 1);
```

Okay, so there was your review of some basic math in the console. Hopefully you already know that much easily because next we introduce a few *new* operators…

Augmented Assignments (Plus Equals, Minus Equals, etc.)

You've already seen mathematical operators used with assignment to a variable like this:

```
let sum = 5 + 2;        // value of sum is 7
```

And you probably recalled that you could alter the value of an existing variable (as long as you don't try to reuse the `let` keyword) like this:

```
sum = sum + 3;          // value of sum is 10 now
```

But now you get to learn another handy little trick. You can use `+=` (pronounced "plus equals") as a shorthand way of making a variable add to itself! This is known as an **augmented assignment** because it first performs an operation on the variable (that's the "augment" part) and then *assigns* the new value to that same variable. Here are some examples (be sure to type all of these):

```
let value = 5;
value += 2;    // value is now 7 (this is the same as value = value + 2;)
value += 3;    // value is now 10 (this is the same as value = value + 3;)
value = value + value;    // 20 (though we could've just written value += value;)
value += value;    // 40 (this is the same as value = value + value;)
```

As you may have guessed, this also works with the other math operators too!

```
value -= 25;    // value is now 15 (same as typing value = value - 25;)
value *= 2;     // value is now 30 (same as value = value * 2;)
value /= 3;     // value is now 10 (same as value = value / 3;)
value; // Response: 10
```

Here are just a few more examples to work through. For each
line, try to guess the answer before you test it in the console:

```
let answer = 0;
answer += 2;
answer *= 30;
answer -= 12;
answer /= 6;
answer *= 7 - 5;
answer += answer;
answer;
answer /= 4;
answer -= answer;
answer;
```

Hopefully that was pretty intuitive (meaning, the responses were
what you expected). If you're still struggling with this concept,
try doing this section again. If you still don't understand it, just move on. There will be plenty of
review to help you get it soon enough.

Increment and Decrement Operators (Plus Plus or Minus Minus)

There are two more handy little shortcuts I'd like you to know. The **increment operator**
is a shortcut for taking a number and *adding* the number 1 to it (sometimes known as
"incrementing"). It looks like this (type in your console):

```
let counter = 0;
counter++;      // add 1 (using the increment operator)
```

And the **decrement operator** is kind of like the opposite. It's a shortcut for taking a number and
subtracting the number 1 from it (a.k.a. "decrementing"). It looks like this:

```
counter--;      // subtract 1 (using the decrement operator)
```

So just to make this concept a little clearer, here are three built-in ways to do the exact same *addition*
operation (in such cases, it's generally preferred to use the increment operator):

```
counter = counter + 1;
counter += 1;
counter++;      // increment operator (preferred way)
```

And here are three built-in ways to do the exact same subtraction operation (in such cases, it's
generally preferred to use the decrement operator):

```
counter = counter - 1;
counter -= 1;
counter--;      // decrement operator (preferred way)
```

The Modulo Operation

Ready for the hard one now? Okay.

Percent sign (%) is for *modding*: `9 % 2;`
Response: `1`

Ever seen that one before? It looks weird to most people at first, but it actually makes good sense and is useful in coding! When used for programming, that percent sign (%)—which is made by typing SHIFT+5 on your keyboard—is called **modulo** (or just *mod*), and we use it to get the **modulus** (remainder) of an **integer division** problem! Got it?

What do you mean you're "Even more confused than before"?! Hmm…okay let me start over with a different explanation…

In school, when you first learned how to divide, your teacher probably gave you division problems that worked out evenly with no remainders, decimals, or fractions. You probably learned things like:

9 / 3 = 3
10 / 2 = 5
8 / 4 = 2

All of these problems are easy to divide. But what if the numbers don't work out perfectly? Like this one:

5 / 2 = ?

You might say "5 divided by 2? That's easy! The answer is 2.5 (two-and-a-half)!" Well, that is *one* way to answer it. But what if decimals or fractions are not an option?

For instance, what if you have 5 people and they're trying to share 2 cars? 2 people fit into each car, but there's 1 person left over (a remainder of 1). You're not just going to cut that person in half (at least…I *hope* you're not!)!

This is an example of something called "Integer Division" (or if you're Fancy Nancy, you might prefer to call it **"Euclidean Division"**). In integer division, you don't make fractions or decimals (integers never have decimal points). You just see how many times one number will evenly divide into another number and round down to the nearest whole integer (number). Anything leftover is known as the *remainder*. So in math class, when you're learning integer division you might have problems like this:

3 / 2 = 1 r1 // in math terms, this is "3 divided by 2 equals 1 with a remainder of 1"
4 / 2 = 2 r0 // in math terms: "4 divided by 2 equals 2 with a remainder of 0"
5 / 2 = 2 r1 // "5 divided by 2 = 2 with a remainder of 1"
6 / 2 = 3 r0 // "6 divided by 2 = 3 with a remainder of 0"
7 / 2 = 3 r1 // "7 divided by 2 = 3 with a remainder of 1"

8 / 2 = 4 r0 // "8 divided by 2 = 4 with a remainder of 0"

Did you follow the logic there? That's how basic integer division works with remainders (instead of fractions). Now, when using modulo (%), you're *only* concerned with the *remainder*. Modulo does the same basic integer division problem, then *ignores* the main result and *only* gives you what's left over (the remainder).

Now let's do the same "basic math" problems we just did only let's use modulo to get the remainder. Type these in the console (only type the part in blue):

```
3 % 2;
```
Response: 1 // "3 / 2 = 1 (this part is *ignored*) with a <u>remainder of 1</u> (*this* part is *returned*)"

```
4 % 2; // Response: 0 // "4 divided by 2 = 2 (ignored) with a remainder of 0 (returned)"
5 % 2; // 1 // "5 divided by 2 = 2 with a remainder of 1"
6 % 2; // 0 // "6 divided by 2 = 3 with a remainder of 0"
7 % 2; // 1 // "7 divided by 2 = 3 with a remainder of 1"
8 % 2; // 0 // "8 divided by 2 = 4 with a remainder of 0"
9 % 2; // 1 // "9 divided by 2 = 4 with a remainder of 1"
```

Do you see how it works? Modulo gives the remainder *and nothing else*. Let's try some more together. Type:

```
6 % 3;
```
Response: 0

Is that what you expected? 6 divided by 3 equals 2, right? Well how much is left over to be the remainder? Nothing! 6 is divided evenly by 3 (no *remainder*), so the modulus is 0.

```
7 % 4;
```
Response: 3

Explanation: 7 divided by 4 (using integer division) = 1 with a remainder of 3.

```
4 % 5;
```
Response: 4

Explanation: 4 divided by 5 (using integer division) = 0 (because "5 goes into 4 *zero times*"). This leaves us with a *remainder* of 4 (the amount left over after the failed attempt to divide 4).

```
15 % 2;
```
Response: 1

Explanation: 15 divided by 2 = 7 (ignored) with a remainder of 1. So the modulus is 1.

Now for these, I'd like you to type each statement in the console, try to guess what the result will be—*before* you press the **ENTER** key—then press **ENTER** to see if you're correct:

```
3 % 3;  // Response: 0
4 % 3;  // Response: 1
5 % 3;  // 2
6 % 3;  // 0
7 % 3;  // 1
8 % 3;  // 2
9 % 3;
10 % 3;
11 % 3;
12 % 3;
13 % 3;
14 % 3;
15 % 3;
16 % 3;
17 % 3;
18 % 3;
```

Did you pick up on any pattern? `0, 1, 2, 0, 1, 2, 0, 1, 2, 0, 1, 2...` That's no coincidence. That pattern would continue even if you tried thousands of `x % 3;` statements. Similar behavior happens with *all* modulus statements actually.

For instance, if you were doing a bunch of modulo 2 operations (`x % 2;` like we did earlier), the responses would go like this:

`0, 1, 0, 1, 0, 1, 0, 1, 0, 1, 0, 1, 0, 1, 0, ...`

If you're doing modulo 4 operations (`x % 4;`), the responses would go like this:

`0, 1, 2, 3, 0, 1, 2, 3, 0, 1, 2, 3, 0, ...`

If you're doing modulo 5 operations (`x % 5`), the responses would go like this:

`0, 1, 2, 3, 4, 0, 1, 2, 3, 4, 0, 1, 2, 3, 4, 0, ...`

So in each modulo operation, you will get a number that is less than the divisor (the 2nd number in the modulus equation).

One last thing: remember how the modulo 2 pattern goes like `0, 1, 0, 1, 0, 1...`? Well, because of this predictable pattern, modulo 2 is a fantastic way to find out if a number is even or odd! Any number that returns a value of `0` after modding by 2 is an even number, and any number that returns a value of `1` is an odd number! For instance:

```
8 % 2;       //     0: so 8 is an even number!
17 % 2;      //     1: so 17 is an odd number!
101 % 2;     //     1: so 101 is an odd number!
5590 % 2;    //     0: so 5590 is an even number!
```

```
41703 % 2;    //    1 : odd number!
826834 % 2;   //    0 : even number!
```

Thanks for sticking with me for that full explanation. It's not an easy concept to explain (my kids tell me this may be the most confusing section in the whole book), but hopefully you understand it now. If not, try this section one more time, and if it's still confusing, then keep moving on and maybe you'll figure it out after we use it for a project!

Follow Along: Picking Teams in Dodgeball

If there's one thing to which developers have given a lot of thought, it's how to avoid the humiliation of being the last kid picked in a game of dodgeball. So today, we're going to do that together. We'll devise a simple, fair way to divide a group of students into even teams.

But first, open a new tab in Chrome, navigate to the all-blank screen and open the console—you should be able to do this in your sleep by now!

Okay then, here's what we know about this game of dodgeball:

- The gym class has 12 kids in it.
- Each kid has a unique Student Identification Number (Student ID), which is an integer between 1 and 12.
- This dodgeball game must contain THREE teams (yeah I know; just go with it) of equal size.
- We must assign each kid to a team based on his Student ID—NOT based on dodgeball skills (or lack thereof)!
- We should use a single statement to tell any kid what team he is on.

So how do we go about this? Well, to begin with, let's name the teams! The whole class took a vote, and the most popular team names were: "Team 1", "Team 2", and "Team 0"! (Did I mention this is not a very imaginative class?)

Next, let's assign a variable in the console for the number of teams:
```
let numberOfTeams = 3;
```

And another variable to represent the Student ID for the first student Andrea:
```
let studentId = 1;
```

BTW, did you notice that the variable `studentId` has a lowercase D? Why isn't the D in uppercase like `studentID`? Well, ID is an **acronym**—shortened words that are usually made from taking the starting letters of other words…like LOL (laugh out loud) or BTW (by the way) or my personal favorite TL;DR (which doesn't apply in the case of this book). The "I" in ID is short for "i" and the "D" is short for "dentification." Anyway, ID is an acronym, and acronyms are most readable in camelCase when they're capitalized the same way as any other normal word. You'll see more like this in the future.

Now for something cool! Remember modulo? Maybe you thought we'd never find a good use for him. Turns out we need him again in the very same chapter! What are the odds?!

This simple one-liner of code will tell our student exactly which team she is on.

```
studentId % numberOfTeams;
```
Response: 1

Team 1! Okay, so far so good. Here comes another student. This student, Terrell, says his Student ID is 2. For the above line of code to work, we'll need to *update* the `studentId` and run it again. Remember, since we're *changing* the `studentId` variable (not creating a new one), we need to NOT have that `let` keyword.

```
studentId = 2;
```

Now that we've changed the `studentId`, we can press the **UP_ARROW** on the keyboard two times to bring back the same line of code from before and run it:

```
studentId % numberOfTeams;
```
Response: 2

Team 2! Now here comes Terrell's best friend Suresh (Student ID of 12). He's hoping to be on the same team as Terrell. We tell him that we don't play favorites, and we don't accept bribes (he didn't bring any candy anyway). We will simply let our program determine the teams. Let's see if we can change the `studentId` and then run the modulo statement in one line! We can do this because there's a semicolon (;) in between the two statements:

```
studentId = 12;   studentId % numberOfTeams;
```
Response: 0

Team 0! Well, Terrell and Suresh don't get to be on the same team, but at least our teams are even so far. Let's assign teams for the rest of the kids in the class. For each of these statements, press the **UP_ARROW** on the keyboard, then change the `studentId` input and press **ENTER** to execute the statement:

```
studentId = 3;   studentId % numberOfTeams;        //    0
studentId = 4;   studentId % numberOfTeams;        //    1
studentId = 5;   studentId % numberOfTeams;        //    2
studentId = 6;   studentId % numberOfTeams;        //    0
studentId = 7;   studentId % numberOfTeams;        //    1
studentId = 8;   studentId % numberOfTeams;        //    2
studentId = 9;   studentId % numberOfTeams;        //    0
studentId = 10;  studentId % numberOfTeams;        //    1
studentId = 11;  studentId % numberOfTeams;        //    2
```

Super! We've now used our program to appropriately assign all students to their respective teams, and nobody's feelings were hurt! (At least...not before being hit in the face with a dodgeball.)

CHAPTER 2: QUIZ

As with any Chapter quiz, I recommend you take it without looking back for any of the answers. Write your answers down in your Workbook (see Ch. 1 Quiz for an explanation of the Workbook). All of the correct answers are in the back of the book. After you finish the quiz, check your answers to see if you missed anything.

1. What does the + symbol mean when doing mathematical operations in JavaScript?

2. In JavaScript, what symbol is used for multiplication?

3. Which data type is this?
   `3456`

4. What does the / symbol mean when doing mathematical operations in JavaScript?

5. What is the data type of the variable `whatTypeAmI` after running this statement?
   ```
   let whatTypeAmI = 5;
   ```

6. What should be used to separate and group different math operations to improve readability and ensure that your operations perform in the order in which you intended?

7. What special symbol could you use to simplify this assignment?
   ```
   myVariable = myVariable * 2;
   ```

8. What symbol is used for modulo in JavaScript?

9. What is the simplest (i.e., shortest) way to write this (using a special symbol)? What is the special symbol called?
   ```
   myVariable = myVariable + 1;
   ```

10. What is the simplest (i.e., shortest) way to write this (using a special symbol)? What is the special symbol called?
    ```
    myVariable = myVariable - 1;
    ```

11. How would you *change* this statement to make it say "three times the sum of 4 plus 1" (Hint: the response should be 15 when run in the console)?
    ```
    3 * 4 + 1;
    ```

12. If you were writing a program to determine if a value was odd or even, what number would you use after the modulo operator?

13. What special symbol could you use to simplify this assignment?
`myValue = myValue - 8;`

14. How many *unique* (i.e., *different*) values could you possibly get if you did a long series of integer operations that all ended in "modulo 5" (example: `11 % 5;` `12 % 5;` `13 % 5;` etc.)?

15. What is the *collective* name for the symbols that first perform an operation on a variable and then *assign* the new value to that same variable (**e.g.** `+=`, `-=`, `*=`, and `/=`)?

16. Suppose you wanted to make a JavaScript program with hundreds of lights following a color pattern of red, blue, green, red, blue, green, red, blue, green, etc. Which mathematical operator might be most useful for you in your program?

CHAPTER 2: KEY CONCEPTS

As with the Key Concepts section of any chapters, glance over this list and if there's anything you don't think you fully understand, look back in the chapter to review it before moving on. These are roughly in the order they were introduced:

- Data Types
- Numbers
- Mathematical Operators
- Parens in mathematical operations
- Augmented Assignments
- Plus Equals
- Minus Equals
- Times Equals
- Divided by Equals
- Increment Operator (++)
- Decrement Operator (--)
- Modulo
- Operator Symbols
- Patterns in Modulo operations
- Finding even and odd

Use these drills in whatever way will help you the most (I recommend putting the answers in your Workbook). Feel free to try each of them in the console and don't hesitate to look in the back of the book if you'd like any help. Even if you already know how to do this, the drills will help you to continually remember these concepts going forward.

A. Try typing these valid code snippets in the console.

1.
```
8 * (7 - 5);
```

2.
```
15 / (6 - 4 + 1);
```

3.
```
(7 + (3 * 1) - 2) / (3 - 1);
```

4.
```
((5 + 3) / (10 - 6)) * 3;
```

5.
```
let sum = 6;
sum *= 5;
sum -= 10;
sum /= 4;
sum += sum * 3;
sum;
```

6.
```
let coinsInMyPocket = 5;
coinsInMyPocket++;
coinsInMyPocket++;
coinsInMyPocket--;
coinsInMyPocket++;
coinsInMyPocket;
```

7.
```
14 % 3;
```

8.
```
(20 - 10) % (8 - 4);
```

9.
```
4 * (500 % 5);
```

10.
```
2018 % 100;
```

11.
```
15 % (3 + 1);
```

12.
```
let numberOfTeams = 4;
let studentIdToAssignToATeam = 17;
let teamNumber = studentIdToAssignToATeam % numberOfTeams;
teamNumber;
```

B. What's wrong with each of these code snippets?

Hint: type some of these in the console to see if any error messages show up to help!

1.
```
let thisNumber % 2 = 0;
```

2.
```
var 1 = 4 % 3;
```

3.
```
let mySpecialValue = 5;
mySpecialValue = mySpecialValue += 6;
```

4.
```
(4 + (3 * 1) % 2;
```

5.
```
let myModValue == 5 % 5;
```

6.
```
let thisModulus = modDividend % modDivisor;
```

7.
```
let anotherModulus = 5 + 2) % 25;
```

8.
```
6 +* 3;
```

9.
```
5 % 25 = theFinalAnswer;
```

10.
```
let greatNumber += 4;
```

11.
```
let newerNumber = 5;
newerNumber * 3 += 6;
```

12.
```
let notTechnicallyAnErrorButProbablyNotVeryUsefulInCoding = 5.25 % 4;
```

13.
```
var ummmWhatAStrangeErrorMessage = 20 +/ 5;
```

CHAPTER 2: **AGGREGATE REVIEW**

This chapter introduces one more new concept that you will see in all future chapters: Aggregate Review. "Aggregate" sorta means "all the separate pieces combined." These drills and questions are like the Chapter Drills or Chapter Quizzes but instead of just reviewing this one chapter, drills/questions in this section may include bits from anything you've learned up to this point.

In future chapters, these will be among the most valuable drills to make sure you haven't forgotten any important concepts. Write down *all* of your answers in your Workbook. As with all drills and questions, feel free to consult the answers at the back of the book!

1. What kind of casing is `thisVariableWithSomeCapitalLettersInIt`?

2. What keyboard shortcut is used for opening up the console in Chrome?

3. Is this a valid statement? (And if not, why not?)
    ```
    var 1stStudentId = 1;
    ```

4. Is this a valid statement? (And if not, why not?)
    ```
    let idForStudentNumber12 = 12;
    ```

5. True/False: Error messages are intended to help.

6.   What kind of error message would result from an open paren that is never closed?

7.   Which mathematical operator would be most useful for checking if a given value is evenly divisible by 6?

8.   What would you type into the URL address bar in order to get a completely empty page in Chrome?

9.   What symbol could you use to make this assignment say the same thing, but shorter?
```
mathyValue = 7 + mathyValue;
```

10.   Is this valid JavaScript? (And if not, why not?)
```
var faveCereal = 'Kix';  faveCereal = 'Froot Loops';  faveCereal;
```

11.   Is this valid JavaScript? (And if not, why not?)
```
let faveCereal = "Cap'n Crunch";
let faveCereal = "Lucky Charms";
faveCereal;
```

DIY: FourSquare

Oh boy! Another "Do It Yourself" project! Remember, all of these DIY projects will use concepts we've learned in this chapter. It also may help to remember that DIY projects are often similar to the chapter's Follow Along project, so that would be a good place to look back if you get stuck.

Here's your mission:

The same gym class from our Follow Along project earlier in the chapter (where every student has a studentId of a consecutive number from 1-12) now wants to play a few simultaneous games of FourSquare. And get this: 4 new students (with studentIds of 13, 14, 15, & 16) have joined the class!

But now the kids can't seem to agree on which FourSquare court each will play on! There are 4 courts (Numbered 0, 1, 2, and 3), and each court has only enough space for exactly 4 students. Because you have proven your brilliance in selecting dodgeball teams, they naturally depend on your leadership for equitably determining which kids will go to which FourSquare court—based on each kid's studentId. Using a similar formula to the one you used in Dodgeball, which court should each of the 16 students play in?

So here are the relevant pieces of information to consider:

   •   The gym class has 16 kids in it.

- Each kid has a unique Student Identification Number (Student ID), which is a number between 1 and 16.
- This four square game must use all 4 courts.
- You must assign each kid to a FourSquare court based on his Student ID.
- You should use a single statement per kid to tell each kid what team he is on.

Close, then open Chrome, navigate to a blank page, open the JavaScript console, and type all of your code in the console. Use variables (with descriptive names like `numberOfCourts`) whenever appropriate. Also, remember to use the **UP_ARROW** key to bring back previous lines in the console. This will make things faster and easier than retyping it all.

If you get stuck, don't just sit there. First, look back at the solution to the Follow Along (Dodgeball) project as the solution to this problem will be *very* similar to that one. If you're still having trouble, go ahead and look at the "Ch. 2 DIY Recommended Solution" in the back of the book. But don't be lazy either! After looking at the answer, cover it back up, and try to work through the entire problem from the beginning without glancing at the answer again until you're done. Repeat this as often as necessary so you'll know you can really do this stuff!

3 COMMENT ON THE STRING SECTION

In the previous chapter, we introduced the concept of data types *in JavaScript. We then went on to give exactly one example of a data type: numbers. You might be thinking at this point that JavaScript is merely used for making computers behave like calculators.*

Well, you might be relieved to know that there are, in fact, other data types. In this chapter, we'll be commenting on perhaps the most useful data type of them all: strings!

And speaking of comments, this would also be a great time to introduce you to *another* valuable JavaScript language construct...

Comments

As a developer, there will be times when you want to write something in your code that is meant only for humans to read—NOT for computers to execute! Perhaps you'll want to make a note to your future self (a.k.a. "Future You") about why you wrote something the way you did. Or maybe you'll want to run most of your code but you'd like the interpreter to skip one line or section. This is where you'll need to use **comment**s. (Reminder: words that are first introduced with bold typeface have definitions in the glossary in the back of the book).

We're going to do some more work in the console. Please close all of your programs again, then open Chrome, go to the blank screen, and open the console (refer to Ch. 1 if you forget any of the shortcuts).

Single-Line Comments

I've actually used **single-line comments** a few times in this book so far, but I was pretty sneaky about it. A single-line comment looks like this (Type this in the console):

```
// Hey! I'm a comment!
```
Response: `undefined`

When the interpreter sees those two forward slashes (//), it will ignore anything from that point until the end of the line. It also works if you have other code on the same line like so:

```
5 + 1; // this is easy... can't I just do this in my head?
3 * 4; // oh I see the point now.
8 + 2; // the interpreter runs the code, but ignores this comment after it
```

Do you see how that works?

Break Returns in the Console

We're just about to do more work with comments, but before you can properly type this next block of code, you'll need to know how to make a break return in the console. A **break return** is just a more technical term for a new line. Normally, when you're typing a document or an email, you press the ENTER key (which, of course, is called the RETURN key on a Mac) whenever you want to make a break return (move the cursor to a new line).

But as you've probably noticed, the ENTER key does something special in the console. It tells the interpreter that you've finished your statement(s), and you'd like to see the response. We've been using the ENTER key in all the previous chapters to see the console response. But what if you just want to move to the next line (i.e., make a "break return")? Well for this, you simply use a key combination: SHIFT+ENTER (hold down the SHIFT key when you press ENTER). Note: there are two SHIFT keys on your keyboard—one on each side—so choose whichever one suits your fancy.

Type this block of code (including the comments) in the console with break returns:

```
// Press SHIFT+ENTER after this comment
var simpleMath = 2 + 2; // make another break return here
simpleMath; // now you can just press ENTER. Console should return 4!
```

If you did this correctly, you should have gotten a response from the console of 4 AND you should have not gotten any `undefined` responses in the middle of your code block. Did that work properly for you? If the console ever said `undefined`, that means you must not have used the SHIFT+ENTER key combination. So if that's the case, try it again and be sure to use that combination to make a break return every time.

Another thing to note: there's nothing exact about the syntax in the comments. Comments are for humans to read, and you can't get syntax errors. Humans are way smarter than computers, so you don't have to get every character correct as long as a human can figure out what you mean.

Another block of code for the console with break returns and single-line comments:

```
// my current salary (rounded up to nearest million)
let myAnnualSalary = 1000000;
// 365 is the number of days in a year
let dailyWage = myAnnualSalary / 365;
dailyWage; // my daily pay (maybe a little exaggerated)
```

We good? You ready to move on? Great! Now, let's finally get to the main point of this chapter: strings!

Block Comments

What?? Block comments? Is this another interruption?! C'mooonnnn!!

Yes, it is. I'll try to keep this short, then we can move on to strings for realz.

Block comments are similar to single-line comments, but instead of the interpreter just ignoring *one* line, it will ignore *every* line until it finds the end of the block comment. Let me explain. Block comments start with /* and end with */. When the interpreter sees /*, it thinks "I will not pay attention to anything else until I see a */". Here's an example (remember to use **SHIFT+ENTER** for the break returns!):

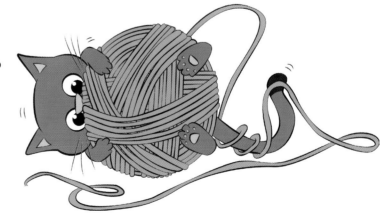

```
/* here's a comment with a
break return. Interpreter will ignore this
until it sees...
*/
4 + 9; /* now this line will run! */
```

Did that work for you? Let's try another one:

```
let faveHero = "Green Lantern";
/* Just kidding!
Nobody's favorite hero is Green Lantern!
faveHero = "Batman"; // will the interpreter read this line of code? NO!
*/
faveHero; // Haha!
/* The console is still fooled because it ignores all these block comments!
I told you computers are not as smart as humans! */
```

Got it now? Okay, there's more that can be said about block comments, but I'm just as eager to get moving on as you are, so let's keep going!

Strings

We touched on **strings** a little bit in the first chapter but I didn't explain it fully because there was already so much else to explain, and I ~~was too lazy~~ didn't want to overwhelm you.

You might use strings more than any other basic data type. When creating a new string, you'll use either 'single quotes' or "double quotes." Here are several examples of strings:

```
"Hello World!"
'Hi'
"You could have one word, an entire sentence, paragraph, or even multiple pages of
text in one string"
'12345'
```

Whoops! How did that last one get in there? How embarrassing! Isn't that a number?!

Actually, no it isn't! It's a *string* because it has single quotes around it! Did I fool you? (...maybe just for a second?)

Pay close attention to your single and double quotes. If you start a string with a single quote ('), you can have double quotes inside it, but it needs to end with another single quote ('). And of course the reverse is true for double quotes ("). If you start with a double quote, you must end with another double quote (").

Now before we get too big for our britches, I think it's about time we make a few mistakes, shall we? But first, I'd like you to fully close (not just minimize) every program on your computer, so you're just looking at the plain desktop. Then follow the steps you memorized from Chapter 1 again until you have the console open.

Ready now? Okay, let's look at a couple errors and how to fix them. Type:

```
let somethingIsWrong = 'Oh My Darlin' Clementine.';
```
Console Response: `Uncaught SyntaxError: Unexpected identifier`

```
""Pop!" Goes the Weasel.";
```
Response: `Uncaught SyntaxError: Unexpected identifier`

Did you catch what was wrong with these statements? If not, look again at your console and pay attention to the code coloring that happened when you typed the single or double quotes. It's very subtle. In the first one, the single quote in `Darlin'` looked to the JavaScript interpreter like it was the CLOSING single quote for the string! Similarly, in the second one, the double quote mark before the `Pop` looked like the closing double quote for the string.

Fortunately, the fix for each of these is simple. Just change the *outer* quotes to be single quotes or double quotes (whichever one you are NOT using in the middle of the string). Like this:

```
let nowItIsFine = "Oh My Darlin' Clementine"; // string is now in double quotes
'"Pop!" Goes the Weasel.'; // string is now wrapped in single quotes
```

Does that make sense? Here are two more examples with single and double quotes used properly in statements. Type:

```
let singleQuotedString = 'Red Says "Stop!" Green Says "Go!"';
let doubleQuotedString = "I've Been Workin' on the Railroad.";
```

Characters

Strings are made up of individual pieces called **character**s. You could just say "letters" but sometimes that might get confusing because a string could also have numbers and symbols in it too. For example:

```
"a"; // one character string
"abc 123"; // 7 character string (space counts as a character too)
"secret_P@ssW0rd!!1"; // 18 character string
```

We also use the term *character* to describe any single letter, number, or symbol that is typed in a *line* of code (even if it's *not* part of a string). Like this:

```
"where is the semicolon?"; // semicolon is the 26th character in this line of code
"where's the apostrophe?"; // apostrophe (') is the 7th character in this line
```

Escaping with Backslash

Now let's shake things up just a bit:

```
let hereComesAnError = 'Say "It ain't so"!';
```
Response: `Uncaught SyntaxError: Unexpected identifier`

Oh dear! The inner string has *both* double *and* single quotes! What are we supposed to do now? Well, thankfully, when you're really in need, there is one friend who always has your back: \\\\\\\\\\\ **BACKSLASH**! \\\\\\\\\\\

The backslash (\) can be found above the **ENTER** key on your keyboard. Some people don't trust your new friend backslash. They're probably afraid that the minute they start to get close, he'll slash them in the back! Well, relax. He's here to help! Here's how to use a backslash in a string:

```
let backslashedString = 'Say "It ain\'t so"!';
let alternateBackslashedString = "Say \"It ain't so\"!";
```

In coding, we call that "escaping." So here's the gist: a string can be surrounded by single quotes or double quotes. Either is fine. But if you want to use the *same* kind of quote marks in the *middle* of the string that you have on the outsides, then you need to **escape** them using a backslash. Got it? Here's a few more exercises to be sure this sinks in:

```
"My doctor said \"Mylanta!\"";
'I ain\'t gonna say "ain\'t" \'cuz "ain\'t" just ain\'t right.';
'Where\'d\'ya think you were goin\'?';
"I can't share my candy because mom said \"No.\"";
```

If you're still struggling with this, play with it a few times in the console before moving on.

Concatenating Strings

I'll now explain another thing we did in Chapter 1. When working with strings (those things with single or double quotes around them, remember?), the plus sign (+) takes on a special meaning. Instead of being used for *adding*, it gets used for *concatenating*! Try these in the console:

```
"Simon" + "says" + "no" + "spaces" + "allowed.";
'But ' + 'spaces ' + 'are ' + 'more ' + 'readable.';
"This " + "sentence " + "has " + 4 + " spaces.";
'Hey! the number "' + 7 + '" is concatenated to this string!';
```

Each of those statements would return a string. That's the data type. If you add two or more *numbers* together you'll get a *number*. If you add (**concatenate**) two or more *strings*, you'll get a *string*. Which data type will you get when you add/concatenate a string with a number (as we did just now)? Another string!

That's why the return values on each of these statements will have the data type of string (you can tell because the response for each has quotes around it). Type:

```
"1"; // string, NOT a number
'1' + '2';
"12" + 3;
'1' + ("2" + "3") + 4;
1 + ("234" + "5");
12 + '345' + 6;
var lastTwoDigits = 67;  "12345" + lastTwoDigits;
'1234567' + (4 * 2);
let startingString = '1234'; startingString += 56 + ("78" + (3 * 3)); startingString;
```

Did you notice the += ("plus equals") in that last statement? In the previous chapter, we showed how += (called an *augmented assignment*) can be used to add a number to a variable and then assign the new value back to the variable. Well, this is doing pretty much the same thing except with strings, which means that instead of "adding," we're "concatenating" (connecting the strings together) and still assigning the resulting value back to the original variable.

In all my years of coding, I don't think I've yet met a software developer who says that string concatenation is his favorite part of the job. It's more like one of those basic skills that you need to get out of the way in order to understand the other stuff. Hopefully, this chapter did that for you.

Follow Along: Famous Author Bio

Now for another fun Follow Along project! But first, please close everything down again and reopen it all to get to a clean console. You may groan now, but in the future, you'll appreciate the fact that all this repetition helped to ensure that you can do this stuff easily, and basic things like opening a blank page to use the console don't trip you up.

Here's the mission:

Following the immense success of his new book *I'll Go Second*, famous author Hugo First wants a dynamic bio for his website. He needs us to build a paragraph listing a few personal details his fans need to know including his name, age, current book title, hobby, and a favorite quote from the latest book. He also wants us to document our code with single-line and block comments (not sure why this matters to him, but whatevs). Lastly, we need to keep the paragraph dynamic with variables so he can use this same paragraph as a template for the other authors at the publishing company!

As with many projects, I like to start by typing out what we know (don't forget to use **SHIFT+ENTER** for the break returns in the block comment!):

```
/*
Variables describing author
(for use in the paragraph)
*/
let authorFirstName = 'Hugo';
let authorLastName = 'First'; // this is only used to create the fullName
// let authorMiddleInitial = 'B'; // commenting this line out; we don't need it.
let authorFullName = authorFirstName + ' ' + authorLastName; // see?
let bookTitle = "I'll Go Second";
let age = 25; // a number, when concatenated to a string, becomes a string
let hobby = 'cliff diving';
let quote = 'If at first you don\'t succeed, maybe cliff diving isn\'t for you.';
```

Now, let's make that full bio and concatenate all the variables we've created here!

```
let bio = authorFullName + ' is the '
    + age + '-year-old author of the bestselling book "'
    + bookTitle + '".  When not writing books, ' + authorFirstName
    + ' enjoys ' + hobby + ' and spending time with the family.  '
    + authorFirstName + '\'s favorite quote from \""
    + bookTitle + '" is "' + quote + '"';
```

You may have noticed all of the varied uses of single quotes, double quotes, and backslashes. I hope that wasn't confusing. I included a variety here just to emphasize the point that you can do this however you please. In general, I personally like to use single quotes for strings in JavaScript when feasible, but I usually use double quotes when the string has an apostrophe in it. Some developers prefer double quotes to be the default for strings. It's really fine either way.

Okay now, let's see if we did that correctly:

```
// display full bio
bio;
```

Response (hopefully): `"Hugo First is the 25-year-old author of the bestselling book "I'll Go Second".  When not writing books, Hugo enjoys cliff diving and spending time with the family.  Hugo's favorite quote from "I'll Go Second" is "If at first you don't succeed, maybe cliff diving isn't right for you.""`

Did you get the proper response? If not, first see if there are any error messages as these can be very helpful in tracking down bugs. Then go back and look carefully at every character you typed to be sure that it is the same as in the book. Pay special attention to the single quotes (apostrophes), double quotes, plus signs, and backslashes.

If that did work properly, try changing some of the variables and see if you can get it to work with a

new book title and author (perhaps the suspense novel *I'm Fine* by Howard Yu)! Remember, that when *changing* existing variables, you must *remove* the `let` keyword from the line (otherwise you'll get a syntax error!).

CHAPTER 3: QUIZ

Write your answers down in your Workbook. Don't look back at the chapter for answers. After you finish the quiz, check your answers against the back of the book (even if you're pretty sure you got them right).

1. Comments in code are intended for the _____ to read.
    a. JavaScript interpreter
    b. human
    c. console

2. Which data type is arguably the most commonly used data type in JavaScript?

3. The JavaScript interpreter will _____ any comments it finds.
    a. execute (run)
    b. compile
    c. ignore

4. What symbol indicates a single-line comment?

5. What is the key combination to create a break return when typing in the console?

6. A JavaScript string is usually surrounded by _____.

7. Which characters must you type to start a block comment?

8. Which characters indicate the end of a block comment?

9. True/False: When dealing with strings, it's generally much better to use double quotes than to use single quotes.

10. A string is made up of one or more individual _____.

11. What does the + symbol mean when working with strings in JavaScript?

12. What single character can you *add* to this statement to avoid a Syntax Error?
    ```
    let movieQuote = 'The name's Bond. James Bond.';
    ```

13. How can you *change* (not add) two existing characters in this next line to avoid a Syntax Error?
```
let differentMovieQuote = 'Here's looking at you, kid.';
```

CHAPTER 3: **KEY CONCEPTS**

As with the Key Concepts section of any chapter, glance over this list and if there's anything you don't think you fully understand, look back in the chapter to review it before moving on. These are roughly in the order they were introduced:

- Purpose of comments
- Single-line comments
- Break returns in the console
- Block comments
- String data type
- Single and double quotes surrounding strings
- Characters
- Backslash to escape characters
- Concatenating strings
- Plus equals operator with strings
- Concatenating numbers with strings

CHAPTER 3: **DRILLS**

A. Try typing these valid code snippets in the console.

1.
```
// Single-line Comment
```

2.
```
/* Block comment.  Remember to use SHIFT+ENTER
when creating break returns in the console. */
```

3.
```
/**********************
* Since block Comments *
* span multiple lines, *
* you can build pretty *
* boxes like this one! *
**********************/
```

4.
```
var faveCandyBar = "Butterfinger"; // Hmm... not sure
faveCandyBar = 'Snickers'; // yeah I like this better
faveCandyBar += ' Fun Size'; // don't overdo it
// faveCandyBar = KitKat; // wrote this, then commented it out later
faveCandyBar; // "Snickers Fun Size" (because "KitKat" line is commented out)
```

5.
```
let singleQuotedString = 'Are we there yet?';
singleQuotedString;
```

6.
```
let threeCharacterString = 'No.'; threeCharacterString;
```

7.
```
let concatenatedString = 'Are we there yet? '
+ 'Are we there yet? ' + 'Are ' + 'we ' + 'there ' + 'yet?';
concatenatedString;
```

8.
```
let doubleQuotedString = "We'll get there when we get there.";
doubleQuotedString;
```

9.
```
let singleQuotedStringWithQuotesInIt = 'But Mom said, "We will '
+ 'be there before you know it"!';
singleQuotedStringWithQuotesInIt;
```

10.
```
let doubleQuotedStringWithBackslashesInIt = "I also said, "
+ "\"Quit pestering your father from the back seat\"!";
doubleQuotedStringWithBackslashesInIt;
```

11.
```
let singleQuotedStringWithBackslashesInIt = 'But I\'m sooooo '
+ 'tired, and I can\'t sleep with my head on the window.';
singleQuotedStringWithBackslashesInIt;
```

12.
```
let concatenatedStringsWithApostrophes = "If you don't quit your whinin'"
+ ", " + "I'm gonna stop this car!";
concatenatedStringsWithApostrophes;
```

B. What's wrong with each of these code snippets?

Hint: Type some of these in the console to see if any error messages show up to help!

1.
```
// let whatCouldGoWrong = 'Uh oh';
whatCouldGoWrong;
```

2.
```
let faveTvShow = 'Miraculous'; /* Cataclysm!
faveTvShow;
```

3.
```
let inTheDaytime = 'I'm Marinette!';
```

4.
```
//* Simply the best
    block comment
**/
```

5.
```
/** another // block comment // ok ? **//
```

6.
```
var upToTheTest = 'when ' + 'things ' * "go " + "wrong!";
```

7.
```
var miraculous = 'the ' + 'luck' + i + 'est';
```

8.
```
let whoLet = "The " + \""dogs\" out?";
```

54

Drills and questions in this section may include bits from anything you've learned up to this point. Feel free to check any code with the console, but also write all answers in your Workbook. After you're done, remember to check your answers against those at the back of the book!

1.   What keyboard shortcut is used for opening up the console in Chrome?

2.   Is this a valid statement? (And if not, why not?)
```
(10 + (4 * 2) - 5) / (6 - 7);
```

3.   Is this a valid statement? (And if not, why not?)
```
let racerNumber8 = 8;
```

4.   What URL address should you go to in order to get an empty page in Chrome?

5.   Is this a valid statement? (And if not, why not?)
```
let validNumber % 4 = 2;
```

6.   True/False: Error messages indicate that something is wrong.

7.   What is a shorter way to write the 2nd line to achieve the same result?
```
let age = 12;
age = 1 + age;
```

8.   Where can a developer type simple JavaScript commands to test them out and get immediate responses.

9.   What kind of error message would result from this code?
```
let letterBeforeM = 'N'; let letterBeforeM = 'L'; letterBeforeM;
```

10.   Is this a valid statement? (And if not, why not?)
```
let dividend = 10;
let divisor = 3;
let remainderStatement = 'The Euclidean division of ' + dividend
    + ' by ' + divisor
    + ' yields a remainder of ' + (dividend % divisor);
remainderStatement;
```

11.   Chrome, Firefox, Internet Explorer, Edge, and Safari are all examples of _____.

12.   What form of capitalization should you use with variable names in JavaScript?

13.   What should be used to separate and group different math operations to improve readability and ensure that your operations perform in the order in which you intended?

14.   Which data type is this?
```
'2000'
```

15. Which data type is this?
```
"A cup of proper coffee from a copper coffee pot"
```

16. What does a single equals sign imply in a statement?

17. What is a shorter way to write this to achieve the same result?
```
let faveEntree = "Chicken";
faveEntree = faveEntree + " Burrito";
```

18. What is the percent sign called when used as a JavaScript operator?

19. Is this valid JavaScript? (And if not, why not?)
```
let faveChips = "Fritos";
// let faveChips = "Doritos";
// faveChips;
```

20. Is this valid JavaScript? (And if not, why not?)
```
/* let favePopcorn = "Butter";
let favePopcorn = "Caramel"; */
favePopcorn;
```

DIY: Your Personal Bio

Word has gotten out that you created the bio paragraph for some famous authors, so now you're becoming quite the celebrity in your own right! As a soon-to-be-uber-famous JavaScript bio creator, everyone now wants to learn about your hobby, your pet, your best skill, your grade in school, and your favorite cartoon movie!

Include variables, single-line comments, block comments, and string concatenation (as you did in the Follow Along project) to create a bio for your now-famous self!

Remember: use that Workbook. If you need help, go ahead and look at the answer in the back. But if you do that, try to look without typing (i.e., don't copy the answer), then go back to the console and try to do it again without looking. Repeat as many times as necessary.

HAVE SOME FUNCTIONS

If you've never learned a programming language before, the name "function" probably doesn't do much for you. But as someone who works with them every day, I am super excited to teach these to you! In fact, in all of the Follow-Along and DIY projects we've done together up to this point, I kept thinking to myself, "The way I *really* want to do this project is with a function, but we haven't discussed functions yet...Patience... Chapter 4 is almost here!" Well, now we're in Chapter 4 (at last!), so let's dive right in!

Functions: the Basics

"But what *is* a function?" I'm glad I asked! In programming, a **function** is a separated block of code that can be called to perform a specific task. Before we go further, close all your programs, then bring up the console again.

Declaring a Function

Here's what a very basic function looks like. When you type this in the console, you'll use the curly braces which are close to the **ENTER** key. Also, remember to use **SHIFT+ENTER** to make the break returns (new lines):

```
function getTheNumberFive() {
    return 5;
}
```

This is known as a function *declaration*. Now that this function is **declared**—introduced into our code—it may be used later. Let's break down each part of it:

- The keyword `function` tells the interpreter that what follows will be a **custom** function (i.e., one that you create yourself; not built-in).
- The camelCased name `getTheNumberFive` is the custom *name* of our function. Custom means this is something we make up ourselves. It doesn't matter to the interpreter what this function is called, but it's usually best to use a name that describes well what the function does.

- The parens (parentheses) are required whenever we make a function. Sometimes there are one or more variable names inside the parens, but for this particular function, they're empty.
- The curly braces—{ and } found above the [and] on the keyboard—surround the body of the function (all the inside stuff).
- The body of the function is *indented* (i.e., tabbed over to the right…usually by clicking the TAB key on your keyboard). This is *by convention* (meaning it's not required, but encouraged) and makes it easier to see what all is *inside* the function.
- The keyword `return` indicates that the value immediately following—called "the return value"—will be passed back (or "returned") to the interpreter whenever this function is called.

You may have noticed that the console's response was `undefined`. This, as you may recall, merely indicates that the console didn't have anything more to tell you. All you did was *declare* the function, so there's nothing to return yet (just like when declaring a variable).

Invoking a Function

Next, we're going to **invoke** the function. *Invoking* a function is a fancy name for *calling* a function. Invoking a function looks like this:

```
getTheNumberFive();
```
Response: 5

By first *declaring* a function, and then later *invoking* the function, we end up with the *return value* of the function we declared.

Function Parameters and Arguments

Let's create another function declaration. This one has a variable name inside the parens. When that's the case, we call that variable a **parameter**. Not all functions have parameters but probably most of them do.

```
function addThree(startingNumber) {
    return startingNumber + 3;
}
```

Now that we've declared this function with a parameter, you can invoke it (i.e., call it) just the same as the previous function except we'll be passing in a *value* to be assigned to that parameter. When we pass in a value to be assigned, that value is called an **argument**:

```
addThree(4);
```
Response: 7

We passed the number 4 as an *argument* into the function. When the function received this argument, it automatically assigned it to the variable name `startingNumber` (since that's the name of the *parameter* in our function declaration). Then in the body of the function, some simple math was done on the parameter and the final value was `return`ed back to us.

Just for fun, try passing in a *string* as the argument. Can you guess what will happen?

```
addThree('My favorite number is ');
addThree('4');
```

Do you think you can explain the difference between parameters and arguments? Here's the difference: *arguments* are the values passed in when the function is invoked (i.e., "called"); those values are then assigned to the *parameters* of the function. Here's another way of putting it: *parameters* are variable names in the function declaration that are waiting to receive values when the function is called; *arguments* are those values that are passed in. Does that make sense now? Good. Lastly, you should also know that many programmers use the two terms (*arguments* and *parameters*) interchangeably. I...even had to look them up when writing this chapter because I forgot which was which.

Let's try declaring a function that expects two strings (note, when using more than one parameter, the parameters must be separated by commas).

```
function heartfeltCompliment(personName, feature) {
    let compliment = 'Wow, ' + personName + '!  Your '
        + feature + ' is looking great today!';
    return compliment;
}
```

When we invoke this function, we'll need to pass in two strings (Remember to use single or double quotes for strings!) as arguments separated by a comma:

```
heartfeltCompliment('Jeremy', 'hair');
```
Response: `"Wow, Jeremy!  Your hair is looking great today!"`

Why thank you, computer! Maybe I should sleep on the left side of the bed more often!

DRY (Don't Repeat Yourself)

One thing that all good developers try to do is to stay **DRY**. That means we follow the principle of D.R.Y.: Don't Repeat Yourself.

Sometimes in our coding, there are patterns that need to be followed over and over again. If we type everything out each time, it can make a simple concept feel overly complicated and hard to read. Functions are great tools for helping us to avoid repeating ourselves.

Here's a silly example to help you understand this concept:

Your Little Sister: How can you tell if a car is red?

You: Well, if the doors are red, the hood is red, the trunk is red, and the frame is red, then it's probably safe to say that the car is red.

Your Little Sister: Okay. But how can you tell if a car is blue?

You: Well, if the doors are blue, the hood is blue, the trunk is blue, and the frame is blue, then it's probably safe to say that the car is blue.

Your Little Sister: Okay. But how can you tell if a car is orange?

You: Well, if the doors are orange, the hood is orange, the trunk is orange, and the frame is orange, then it's probably safe to say that the car is orange.

Your Little Sister: Okay. But how can you tell if a car is lavender?

You: Well, if the doors are lavender, the hood is lavender, the trunk is lav…hmm…I seem to be repeating myself a lot…How many colors are you planning to ask about, sis?

Your Little Sister: I'm not sure yet. How many are in this box of crayons?

Did you notice how repetitive this exchange was becoming? This would be a good time to create a custom function for your little sister (little sisters LOVE custom functions!). Remember to use **SHIFT+ENTER** for the break returns!

```
function howCanYouTellIfACarIs(color) {
    return "Well, if the doors are " + color
        + ", the hood is " + color
        + ", the trunk is " + color
        + ", and the frame is " + color
        + ", then it's probably safe to say that the car is " + color + ".";
}
```

Now, whenever she needs to know this answer, she can call the function and just pass in any color that she finds in her Crayoba Ultimate Big Box of crayons! Let's try a few together. Each time you want to reuse the function, just click the **UP_ARROW** to bring back the previous line of code and change the argument to a different string:

```
howCanYouTellIfACarIs('gray');
```
Response: `"Well, if the doors are gray, the hood is gray, the trunk is gray, and the frame is gray, then it's probably safe to say that the car is gray."`
```
howCanYouTellIfACarIs('cerulean');
howCanYouTellIfACarIs('aquamarine');
howCanYouTellIfACarIs('burnt sienna');
howCanYouTellIfACarIs('robin\'s egg blue');
howCanYouTellIfACarIs('macaroni and cheese');
howCanYouTellIfACarIs('crushed vermillion'); // Disney channel, anyone?
```

Now that's a lot shorter and easier to read isn't it? With this function, you can now keep your little sister well informed and entertained for hours, and you don't have to keep repeating yourself. What a good older sibling you are!

You may have noticed that even with the function call doing most of the work, there is still quite a bit of repetition happening here. Why can't we just enter the entire box of crayon names into one

function and get all of the answers instead of having to call the function over and over for every crayon name? If you thought that, then you are definitely thinking like a software engineer! We can do that with ease…in Chapter 9. When we start talking about *arrays* and *loops*, you'll see how we can create some terrific timesaving functions, and we'll be DRY-er than ever before!

Built-in Functions

alert()

We showed examples of some basic functions that you built yourself, but did you know that there are some functions that JavaScript has already built for you? These are baked right into the language, so you can use these functions whenever you like. We call these **built-in** functions, and they're super useful!

Go ahead and open a new tab in Chrome, then open up the console on a blank page, and let's try these puppies out together!

```
alert('Boo!');
```

Did I scare you? You'll notice that this follows the same format as the functions you created yourself (camelCased word followed by parens and an argument passed in). But there's one major difference: you didn't have to declare this function. The JavaScript language already created it for you. A few more times to be sure we got it:

```
alert('Is this necessary?');
alert("If this were on a real website, wouldn't it be annoying?");
alert('Okay, you\'ve had your fun.');
alert('Hey!  Cut it out!');
```

I'll be honest with you: most users (and developers) dislike the `alert()` function. They find the popup annoying. It can be fun to play with our newfound superpowers a few times. Just be aware, that the `alert()` function is a prime case of using your powers for evil. Don't be drawn in by the dark side!

console.log()

Let's try using our powers for good instead! Here's a sneaky way to **log** information into the `console` (i.e., display typed out info in the console window) so that only coders can read it (remember, most people don't even know that the console exists!).

```
console.log('Top Secret!  For developers only!');
```

As the function name might imply, we call this "logging a message into the console." This is a good power that developers use constantly! When you received error messages in earlier chapters (or maybe in this one if you made some mistakes), you saw an example of the JavaScript Interpreter `logging` messages into the console so you could read them. Pretty useful, huh? You'll use the `console.log` function many more times, so memorize this one!

```
console.log('Log any message you like');
console.log('just pass in a ' + "string");
let message = 'I can pass in a variable as an argument too!';
console.log(message);
let thingToSave = 'day';  console.log('I\'m here to save the ' + thingToSave);
```

While you're logging messages to the console, there's another trick I'd like to show you. And it uses our old friend Backslash! You can use \n to create a new line like this:

```
console.log('Your text can span\n multiple\n lines.');
console.log("Here's the first line.\nHere's the 2nd Line.\n3rd\n4th\n5th!");
```

The \n has many practical business uses, such as creating teddy bear ASCII art in the console. Try typing this with me all on a single line in the console (carefully type each character and space like you're entering a password--notice the double/triple spaces):

```
console.log("  c___c\n  /. .\\\n  \\_T_/\n /'    '\\\n(/  .  \\)\n /';-;'\\\n()/   \\()");
```

Do you see why that works? Every \n creates a new line in the console so you can add more symbols to the line below it. And *voila*! You have ~~made a valuable contribution to society~~ drawn a cute teddy bear!

```
> console.log("  c___c\n  /. .\\\n  \\_T_/\n /'    '\\\n(/  .  \\)\n /';-;'\\\n()/   \\()");
    c___c
   /. .\
   \_T_/
  /'    '\
 (/  .  \)
  /';-;'\
  ()/   \()
```

Math.random()

Here's another useful built-in function: `Math.random()`. Notice that this one starts with an uppercase letter 'M'. There's a reason for this, but we're not going to get into it. Much like in English, there are exceptions to many rules. This is one of them. All of the variables *you* write while using this book will begin with a lowercase letter though. Just remember that the casing matters, so it won't work if you don't capitalize it exactly the right way:

```
Math.random();
Math.random();
Math.random();
Math.random();
```

A different number every time! This function actually returns a random number between 0 and 1 every time. You'll find this helpful at times when you want some randomization.

Math.floor()

The `Math.floor()` function accepts a number as the argument and rounds it *down* to the nearest *integer* (number that doesn't have a decimal point).

```
Math.floor(10.4);
Math.floor(5);
Math.floor(214.19723);
let almost33 = 32.99;  Math.floor(almost33);
```

Put It Together

Let's try mixing a few of our functions together and see if we can get some useful things. You can skip the //comments if you like, but use **SHIFT+ENTER** to make break returns (new lines) so that all of this is typed in the console before you press **ENTER** to submit it (that's important for the next part—all of this must be one big block of code):

```
let randomNumberBetween0And1 = Math.random();
// Multiply 100 times a number between 0 and 1 to receive a number between 0 and 100
let bigRandomNumber = randomNumberBetween0And1 * 100;
// Use Math.floor() to round this number DOWN to the nearest integer ("int")
let bigRandomInt = Math.floor(bigRandomNumber);
let pickNumber = 'Pick a number between 0 and 100: ';
console.log(pickNumber + bigRandomInt);
```

Hopefully you understood every step of that. If not, then read it again very carefully to see if it makes sense. If it still doesn't, try rereading the whole "Built-in Functions" section again. If you still don't understand it, then keep going on to the end of the chapter, and hopefully after the review section, it'll become clearer to you.

Now I'd like you to do something that will cause an error. Press the **UP_ARROW** to get the same large block of code again from before. Then press the **ENTER** key to submit it again. If you've been following along, you should get this error:

```
Uncaught SyntaxError: Identifier 'randomNumberBetween0And1' has already been declared
at <anonymous>:1:1
```

Do you know why we're getting this error? If you're about to say "No," let me stop you and ask, "Did you actually *read* the error message?" Remember, *error messages are our friends*. They're here to help. Read those things!

If you did read the message, you'll probably discover that the culprit is the *first* character on the *first* line (hence why the error message references `:1:1`). The keyword `let` should only be used for creating *new* variables, but we're trying to use it with a variable name that has already been declared once.

You already know one way to fix this (remove the `let` keyword), but I'm going to show you a *new* way. Pay close attention to this part. Press the **UP_ARROW** to bring back that chunk of code again. This time, I want you to add a closing curly brace `}` to the bottom of the chunk of code (after the final `;`). Then use the arrow keys to move the cursor to the top of the chunk of code (using **SHIFT+ENTER** to create a new line), and type this:

```
function logRandomNumber() {
```

So, just to be perfectly clear, after all of these instructions, the console should look like this:

```
function logRandomNumber() {
let randomNumberBetween0And1 = Math.random();
let bigRandomNumber = randomNumberBetween0And1 * 100;
let bigRandomInt = Math.floor(bigRandomNumber);
let pickNumber = 'Pick a number between 0 and 100: ';
console.log(pickNumber + bigRandomInt);
}
```

Now press **ENTER** to get the `undefined` response message. What you've done is taken a block of code and wrapped it in a new custom *function declaration*. You've given it a name. Now you can call this function whenever you like by simply typing:

```
logRandomNumber();
```

Try it yourself several times. You should get a different result every time:

```
logRandomNumber();
logRandomNumber();
logRandomNumber();
```

Did that work for you? I hope so! There was a lot of code in there, so if you didn't get the results you were expecting, look very closely to be sure that every character you typed is correct. Paying close attention to exact detail is a crucial skill for any software developer. "Close enough" is not enough!

Follow Along: Time Machine Instructions

It's Follow Along time! Remember to start by closing down all your programs until you only see the desktop. Then bring back the console from a blank page (also expand the console so you'll have maximum room to write).

Professor Brainsley Von Geniusberg has nearly finished his finest invention yet—a time machine for his cat, dog, ferret, and parakeet! He has already calibrated the chrono-shifters, decarborated the base plate, retrofitted the turbo encabulator, and surmounted the pre-farbed amulite with a malleable logarithmic casing. So the hardest part is already done!

The one thing Professor Von G. still needs is a method for determining which year in time (sometime between 0 A.D. and 2500 A.D.) to send each of the pets. He can't reliably allow each pet to decide this for herself because the professor's animal translator is still in the shop. As he doesn't want to be accused of playing favorites, the professor wishes the process to be randomized. He hasn't read my book to learn randomization techniques yet, so he needs your help! Oh, and this needs to be repeatable so that the pets can take frequent trips to random time periods whenever they wish.

Here's what we know:

- We must determine a year in time between 0 and 2500 A.D.
- This should be a repeatable operation.

To begin, let's create a function together and fill it with hard-coded values (i.e., values that don't change on their own):

```
function timeTravel() {
    let pet = 'cat';
    let year = 1950;
    return 'Your ' + pet + ' is traveling through time to the year ' + year + '!';
}
```

Now that we've declared this function, we can call it many times… \but the problem is that it always returns the same message. Try it:

```
timeTravel();
timeTravel();
timeTravel();
```

To make this dynamic, let's first add the `pet` variable as a parameter (inside the parens):

```
function timeTravel(pet) {
    let year = 1950;
    return 'Your ' + pet + ' is traveling through time to the year ' + year + '!';
}
```

Now, when we call it, we can pass the `pet` as an argument into the function like this:

```
timeTravel('dog');
timeTravel('parakeet');
timeTravel('ferret');
```

Now we're able to send different animals through time, but the time period is always `1950`. Now I like a good sock hop as much as the next guy, but a little variety would be nice. We could fix this in the same way we did with the `pet` by putting the `year` variable in as a parameter. But this would mean that the year would need to be provided manually each time the function is called (such as `timeTravel('cat', 2250);`), which would of course leave the professor open to accusations of playing favorites, so this is out of the question.

Let's fix this by including some randomization in the function. To do this, we need to take `Math. random()`—which you may recall will always give us a random number between `0` and `1`—and multiply it by the highest value we will accept (the year `2500` A.D.):

```
function timeTravel(pet) {
    let maxYear = 2500; // latest possible year we'll accept
    let year = Math.random() * maxYear;
    return 'Your ' + pet + ' is traveling through time to the year ' + year + '!';
}
```

Let's try it now:

```
timeTravel('dog');
timeTravel('ferret');
```

Oooh, we're so close, I can almost taste it! The only problem now is that the number for our `year` still has a decimal point in it! Remember how to shave off that decimal point? Add in `Math. floor()`! We can even put it right in the string concatenation if we want!

```
function timeTravel(pet) {
    let maxYear = 2500; // latest possible year we'll accept
    let year = Math.random() * maxYear;

    return 'Your ' + pet + ' is traveling through time to the year '
        + Math.floor(year) + '!';
}
```

Now try invoking it several times in different ways with different animals!

```
timeTravel('cat');
timeTravel('parakeet');
console.log(timeTravel('dog'));
console.log(timeTravel('ferret'));
alert(timeTravel("pair o' cleats"));
alert(timeTravel('neighbor\'s cat'));
```

Congratulations on literally making history!

One more note: Notice how in those last four examples, you're actually calling a function inside of another function! These are referred to as **nested** functions (one function is inside of another just like a smaller bird's nest might fit inside of a bigger nest) and are very common in JavaScript. When dealing with nested functions, the interpreter will always **evaluate** the functions from the inside out. To evaluate a function means to process the function—run it, invoke it, get the return value from it. So to "evaluate functions from the *inside out*" means the interpreter (the computer) looks at and runs the inner function first.

In one of the examples above, the inner function was `timeTravel('neighbor\'s cat')`. The interpreter runs (evaluates) that function *before* running the outer `alert()` function. After running the inner `timeTravel` function, it takes the `return` value of the inner function (in our case, the `return` value was a string describing the pet's travel status) and passes that `return` value (string) as the argument for the outer `alert()` function.

Did that make complete sense to you? If not, read those last two paragraphs slowly and carefully two more times before moving on. This is an important concept, so do your best to understand it. Now it's quiz time!

CHAPTER 4: QUIZ

Write your answers down in your Workbook. Don't look back at the chapter for answers. After you finish the quiz, check your answers against the back of the book.

1. What is the name for a separated block of code that can be called to perform a specific task?

2. Which symbols surround the body of a function?

3. After creating a function, I can use it later. Calling the function is referred to as _____ the function.

4. What kind of capitalization should be used for function names?

5. What part of the function *sends something back* when the function is called?

6. At the top of a function declaration, there may be variable names (called _____) inside of parens. When invoking this function, values (called _____) may be passed-in to be assigned to these variables.

7. What is the acronym used to describe the intention of good developers to avoid writing similar blocks of code over and over again?

8. Which of the four built-in functions discussed in this chapter would probably annoy users if they encountered it several times on a website?

9. If passing multiple values into a function, what symbol is used to separate them?

10. Which built-in function is good for sending secret messages to developers (or to yourself while you're debugging your own website) that users probably won't see?

11. Even if a function accepts no input, it still needs what symbols in order to use it?

12. The built-in randomization function returns a value that is greater than _____ but less than _____.

13. Which built-in function rounds any number down to the nearest integer?

14. True/False: A function can be wrapped inside another function.

15. True/False: When evaluating nested function calls, the interpreter will evaluate them from the inside out.

16. True/False: When dealing with nested functions, the interpreter will use the <u>parameter</u> from the inner function and pass it as an argument to the outer function.

17. Which key on the keyboard is used for indenting your code (for example, inside the body of a function)?

18. What do you type in order to create a new line in the console?

CHAPTER 4: **KEY CONCEPTS**

Read this list and look back in the chapter to review anything you're not solid on before moving on:

- What is a function?
- Declaring functions
- Syntax and naming for each part of a function
- Return value
- Invoking functions
- Function parameters
- Passing arguments to functions
- D.R.Y.
- Built-in Functions
- `alert()`
- `console.log()`
- `Math.random()`
- `Math.floor()`
- Nested functions

A. Try typing these valid code snippets in the console

Note: You can paraphrase or even ignore the //`comments`... don't need to be exact on those as long as you're sure you understand them.

1.
```
function getTheWeather() {
    return 'Sweltering with scattered snow flurries';
}
```

2.
```
// Today's weather forecast
getTheWeather();
```

3.
```
/*
Now we'll log the weather
to the console
*/
function logWeather() {
    let forecast = 'cloudy with a chance of meatballs';
    let weatherMessage = "Today's weather is " + forecast;
    console.log(weatherMessage);
    return forecast;
}
```

4.
```
alert('The weather forecast says: \n' + logWeather());
```

5.
```
function whatIsYourName(name) {
    let message = 'Your name is \n' + name;
    console.log(message);
    alert(message);
    return message;
}
```

6.
```
whatIsYourName('<type_your_actual_name_here>');
```

7.
```
function yourFavoriteToy(faveToy, age) {
    return 'You are ' + age + ', and you still enjoy ' + faveToy + '?';
}
```

8.
```
yourFavoriteToy('<your_favorite_toy_here>', '<your_age>');
```

9.
```
function getRandomSingleDieRoll() { // get 6-sided die roll
    /* we need to add 1 because otherwise Math.floor() will
    give us a number between 0 and 5 */
    return Math.floor(Math.random() * 6) + 1;
}
```

10.
```
getRandomSingleDieRoll(); // try this several times to ensure it works
```

11.
```
function getRandomDiceRoll() { // get result of two 6-sided dice
    let die1 = getRandomSingleDieRoll(); // using above function
    let die2 = getRandomSingleDieRoll();
    let sum = die1 + die2;
    console.log('You rolled ' + sum + '! (' + die1 + ' & ' + die2 + ')');
```

```
      return sum;
  }
```

12.
```
alert(getRandomDiceRoll()); // try several times (look at console message)
```

B. What's wrong with each of these code snippets?

1.
```
function noDeclarationNeeded();
```

2.
```
function whoNeedsEm()
    return "It's fine.";
```

3.
```
function dentistOffice() [
    console.log('You may need braces');
]
```

4.
```
function areDonutsTasty() {
    return 'Yes!';
}
areDonutsTasty(console.log());
```

5.
```
console.log('Integer between 0 and 1: ' + Math.random(Math.floor()));
```

6.
```
alert('Users love alert messages!');
```

7.
```
console.log('Random value: ' + Math.random();)
```

8.
```
function getColor {
    return 'purple';
}
console.log(getColor());
```

9.
```
function faveFancyRestaurant() {
    return 'My favorite restaurant is ' + restaurant;
}
faveFancyRestaurant('McDonald\'s');
```

CHAPTER 4: AGGREGATE REVIEW

1. Which data type is surrounded by either single or double quotes?

2. What are the two keywords we've shown that may be used to declare a new variable?

3. True/False: Comments are ignored by the JavaScript interpreter

4. Is this a valid statement? (And if not, why not?)
```
var whyWas6AfraidOf7 = 'because 7 ate 9';
```

5. What single character can you *add* to this statement to avoid a Syntax Error?
```
let lovelySong = 'They Can't Take That Away From Me.';
```

72

6. True/False: Functions are effective tools for following the W.E.T. principle of coding.

7. Does this appear to accomplish the developer's intention? (And if not, why not?)
```
let daysInAYear = 365; /* we'll use this later
```

8. Which data type is this?
```
0
```

9. What symbol is used for single-line comments?

10. A JavaScript string is made up of individual _____.

11. What symbol is used for modulo?

12. True/False: A string should not contain double quotes inside it unless single quotes are used on the outside (surrounding the string).

13. What is a developer trying to arrive at when he/she uses modulo in an operation?

14. True/False: Error messages are for humans to read.

15. What is the color of grass?

16. Where can a developer type simple JavaScript commands to test them out and get immediate responses?

17. Is this a valid statement (feel free to type it in the console)? (And if not, why not?)
```
function getRemainder(dividend, divisor) {
    let remainderStatement = 'The Euclidean division of ' + dividend
        + ' by ' + divisor
        + ' yields a remainder of ' + (dividend % divisor);
    return remainderStatement;
}
getRemainder(10, 3);
```

18. Which mathematical operator would be most useful for checking if a given value is evenly divisible by 325?

19. What special symbol could you use to simplify this assignment?
```
largeNumber = largeNumber + 19;
```

20. Which data type is this?
```
'75'
```

21. Is this valid JavaScript? (And if not, why not?)
```
function requiredAge(5) {
    // must be at least 5 to ride;
    return 5;
}
requiredAge(5);
```

22. What does the key combination **SHIFT+ENTER** do in the console?

23. What key should you press to indent your code inside a function?

24. Is this correct? (And if not, why not?)
```
function giveRandomNumber(min, maxNumber) {
    return Math.floor(Math.random() * maxNumber);
}
giveRandomNumber(20); // looking for a number less than 20
```

25. If you call a function inside of another function, the inner function is said to be _____ within the outer function.

DIY: Town Lottery

Your town wants you to be in charge of choosing this year's lucky lottery numbers! It's very important to each person involved that the numbers be totally random. There are 3 number slots, and each entry has picked some one- or two-digit number between 0 and 99 (i.e., any integer less than 100). So an example of a ticket might be `25-4-92`, or `46-81-7`, or `18-60-98`, etc.

The town needs you to create one single function that will randomly return all three numbers separated by dashes and `log` a message to the console with this result. Good luck! Actually, *you* probably won't need luck, but those lottery players just might!

Remember: if you're struggling with this concept, check the back of the book for help! But then cover up the answer and try doing it all yourself.

5 SHALL I COMPARE?

This chapter has a lot of new information, but it shouldn't be too hard as everything is focused around a simple theme: True & False.

Up to this point, we've discussed two different primitive data types: *numbers* and *strings*. You might not have seen the word **"primitive"** in coding before. It basically means that these data types are not objects (something you'll learn in a future chapter) and have no methods (functions) in themselves.

In this book, we'll discuss all 5 of the different primitive data types (okay technically, there's a 6th one, but it's confusing, and you won't need it for years; so we're just going to pretend there are only 5). Some good news: the last three data types are the easy ones!

Booleans

The third primitive data type you need to know is called a **"boolean"** (rhymes with "truly inn"). The value of a boolean is always either `true` or `false`. That's it! Nothing in between. Either he's telling the truth or he's not. The light is on or it's off. Either it *is* or it *isn't*. You either finished your homework or you didn't.

We're now going to go through *all* of the possible boolean values, and you'll get a chance to type them *all* into the console! Close down all your windows and open the console back up again to type along with these boolean statements (no quotes here):

```
true;
false;
```

Did you get all that? Those are all of the possible values a boolean may contain. Go ahead and review them if you need to. Then let's move along.

Chapter 5

Comparison Operators

Booleans become much more useful when we're comparing things in JavaScript. That's when we can call on our highly skilled team of **comparison operators**.

We'll show a total of eight comparison operators here, but the thing to remember is that no matter which of these operators we're using and no matter which way we use them, we will always end up with a result that is a boolean: either `true` or `false`. Let's type some together in the console. Don't be lazy. Actually type *all* of these—as you should with *everything* in this book that's written in blue text—and watch the console responses to make sure you get the same answers I put here:

"Triple Equals", a.k.a. "Equals Equals Equals" (===):

```
'my house' === "my house"; // true
1 === true; // false
false === false; // true
false === 0; // false
"That's confusing" === 'That\'s confusing'; // true
3 === 3; // true
3 === '3'; // false
```

Notice that last one. `===` means "exactly equal to". It checks if the value is the same *and* the type is the same. In the case of `3 === '3'`, the value is the same, but the data type is not. One is a number while the other is a string.

"Double Equals", a.k.a. "Equals Equals" (==):

```
3 == 3; // true
3 == '3'; // true
0 == 'zero'; // false
1 == true; // true
5 == true; // false
false == 0; // true
```

Did any of those surprise you? `==` means "pretty much equal to". So `false` is *pretty much equal to* `0`, and `3` is *pretty much equal to* `"3"` even though they're different types.

"Not Equals Equals", a.k.a. "Bang Equals Equals" (!==):

```
5 !== 8; // true
true !== 1; // true
```

78

```
0 !== false; // true
"That's confusing" !== 'That\'s confusing'; // false
3 !== 3; // false
3 !== '3'; // true
```

In coding, the exclamation point (!) is sometimes called a "bang" and it always means "not." It's a way of taking the negation (or opposite) of something. So !== will always give you the opposite of ===. Just like ===, it pays attention to data types as well as values. You might read it as "NOT *exactly* equal to".

"Not Equals," a.k.a. "Bang Equals" (!=):

```
5 != 8; // true
true != 1; // false
0 != false; // false
3 != 3; // false
3 != '3'; // false
```

Hopefully this one was pretty intuitive. != always gives you the opposite of the result you would get from ==. You might read it as "NOT even *pretty much* equal to."

To help you better understand the difference between !== and !=, imagine your teacher put this statement on the board:
    "True/False: The number 1 is NOT exactly equal to true." (`1 !== true`)
If you're clever, you'd say that's a `true` statement. On the other hand, the teacher might change the statement to read thusly:
    "True/False: The number 1 is NOT even *pretty much* equal to true." (`1 != true`)
You would have to say that is now a `false` statement as these values *are* pretty much equal to one another (in coding, at least) even though they're different data types.

One more thing: while I want you to understand what == and != do (because you might see them in code), I don't want you to *ever* use them in your own JavaScript code. Why not? Because there's *never* a good reason to. Any scenario where you might use them could instead use the stricter versions: === or !==. If you find that you actually *want* to be more lenient (for instance, if you want to accept a 1 or a '1' or a value of `true`), then you can explicitly write your code to allow for all of these values (using ===), and it is easier for developers reading it to know your intentions instead of assuming that you're just writing a sloppy shorthand. Don't worry if you don't fully understand the reasoning behind this yet (you will in the future), just remember this one simple rule: *Never ever* use == or !=.

"Greater Than" (>):

```
8 > 5; // true
3 > 5; // false
'8' > 5; // true
2 > 2; // false
```

This is probably an easy concept to understand. The "greater than" sign (`>`) tests if the value on the left side of the comparison is larger—greater—than the value on the right. If so, `true`. If not, `false`.

"Less Than" (`<`):

```
8 < 5; // false
3 < 5; // true
2 < 2; // false
```

Another easy one. The "less than" sign (`<`) tests if a *smaller* value is on the left side of the comparison. If that value is smaller, then this resolves to `true`. Otherwise, it's `false`.

"Greater Than or Equal To" (`>=`):

```
8 >= 5; // true
3 >= 5; // false
2 >= 2; // true
```

Another simple one. This is exactly the same as "greater than" except it will *also* resolve to the boolean true if the two values are equal.

"Less Than or Equal To" (`<=`):

```
8 <= 5; // false
3 <= 5; // true
2 <= 2; // true
```

And last but not least is the "less than or equal to" comparison operator (`<=`) which works exactly like "less than" except it also resolves to `true` if the two compared values are equal.

Quick recap: you've now learned all 8 of the comparison operators, which test for equality, inequality, or greatness comparison. There are 6 that you will use frequently in your JavaScript coding career: `===`, `!==`, `<`, `<=`, `>`, and `>=`. And there are two that you will see in other people's code but never use in your own code: `==` and `!=`.

Do you remember what each one does? If you're not sure what all 8 of these do, go back and read once more the section explaining it and try several examples—including any examples you can think of yourself—in the console. Remember, "getting through" a book is meaningless. What matters is what goes in your head. Go as slow as you need to go, but focus on getting this information into your head.

Conditionals

It might be tempting to think that booleans are such a simple concept that they may not be very useful in coding. Actually, booleans are used constantly and usually in the form of conditionals.

What is a Conditional?

That's a good question! A **conditional** statement in coding is used to perform certain blocks of code based on a given **condition**. The condition (for example, a comparison operator like `x === y`) results in a boolean value (`true` or `false`). If the boolean value is `true`, the code is executed (run). Otherwise, the code block is skipped over (doesn't run). Let's look at a practical example.

The `if` Statement

The most common example of a conditional in JavaScript is the `if` statement. Type these:

```
if (true) {
    console.log('the boolean value in parens is true!  this code will run!');
}

if (false) {
    console.log('the boolean value is false; won\'t be logged to the console.');
}
```

The `if` statement checks for a boolean value inside the parens to determine whether or not to run the code inside the block. Seems simple enough right? It also works with variables that resolve to boolean values like this:

```
let booleanVariable = true;
if (booleanVariable) {
    console.log("Hopefully it's no surprise that this code block runs.");
}
```

Truthy and Falsy

It can even work if the value is *not* a boolean. In these next examples, the variables are not booleans (so they're not *exactly* `true` or `false`). But we can say that they're more generally **"truthy"** or **"falsy."** So if you use these inside the parens of an `if` block, they will resolve in the same way as actual boolean values (`true` or `false`). Try these with me:

```
let truthyValue = 1; // still truthy, even though it's a number (not a boolean)
if (truthyValue) {
    console.log('It\'s truthy!');
}

if (0) { // zero is a number (not boolean) but its value is falsy
    console.log('Not going to run this');
}

if ('a string of any positive length is truthy') {
    console.log('works!');
}

if ('') { // this string is empty, so it is falsy
    console.log('nope.'); // this will not run
}

if (-3) { // all integer numbers (except zero) are truthy
    console.log('Yes!');
}
```

Comparison Operators in `if` Statements

So far in this chapter, you've learned about comparison operators and about `if` statements. But we haven't yet put them together. But comparison operators and `if` statements are meant to be together: like cars and tires or printers and ink!

Open the console in a new `about:blank` tab in Chrome. Then let's do these together:

```
// comparisons resolve to boolean values.  will this be true or false?
let comparison = 3 < 9;
if (comparison) {
    console.log('will this line of code be run?');
}

if ('string' === "string") { // put comparison operator right in the parens
    console.log('are they EXACTLY the same?');
}

if (4 !== '4') { // this will resolve to true if these are not identical
    console.log('is it true?');
}

// the if block can be entirely on one line if you like
if (8 <= 7) {console.log('is 8 less-than-or-equal-to 7?');}

if ('abc' > '') {console.log('is short string greater than an empty string? Yes!');}

let numberOfKidsOnTeam1 = 5;
let numberOfKidsOnTeam2 = 6;
if (numberOfKidsOnTeam1 < numberOfKidsOnTeam2) {
    console.log('Team 1 is outnumbered!');
}
```

if...else

The `if` statement is great when you want some code to run only *if* the given condition is `true`. But a good operative understands that he usually must have a backup plan. That is when we get to use another conditional: `if...else`.

```
let doYouLikeGreenEggsAndHam = false;
if (doYouLikeGreenEggsAndHam) {
    console.log("You could eat them with a goat!"); // skip this
} else {
    console.log("Could you would you on a train?"); // run this
}
```

If the condition is `true` (or truthy), the interpreter will run the block of code inside the top part. If the condition resolves `false` (or falsy), it will run the code in the `else` block section.

Now let's change the value and try again. Press **UP_ARROW** to bring up previous code snippets and make changes as needed:

```
doYouLikeGreenEggsAndHam = true; // don't use let keyword
if (doYouLikeGreenEggsAndHam) {
    console.log("You could eat them with a goat!"); // now this will run!
} else {
    console.log("Could you would you on a train?"); // not this
}
```

Wrap it in a Function

Let's wrap some of this `if...else` logic into a function! Do you remember how to define a function? Try this (include the `//TODO:` comment as that tells what we still need "to do"):

```
function mayIOrderAKidsMeal() {
    //TODO: add guts of the function later
}
```

Now you've defined a function! Only problem is that there is nothing in it. Press the **UP_ARROW** key and replace the `//TODO:` comment to fill in the guts (the middle part) of the function like so:

```
function mayIOrderAKidsMeal() {
    let maxAgeToOrderKidsMeal = 10;
    let customerAge = 11; // you may use your real age here if you like
    if (customerAge <= maxAgeToOrderKidsMeal) {
        console.log("You may order a kid's meal!");
    } else {
        console.log('Sorry.  You need to order from the adult menu.');
    }
}
```

Now *invoke* the function by typing its name with parens after it like this:

```
mayIOrderAKidsMeal();
```
Response: `"Sorry.  You need to order from the adult menu."`

Bummer! We missed it by just one year!

But wait! What if a younger kid asks this question? *Then* what will the answer be?

```
let youngKidAge = 5;
mayIOrderAKidsMeal();
```
Response: `"Sorry.  You need to order from the adult menu."`

Are you kidding me?! You're gonna turn down a 5-year-old kid who merely wants to order from the kid's menu?! How could such a travesty happen?!

Well the problem is that our function is hardcoded with the `customerAge` set to `11`. We should fix this in the function declaration itself. Press the **UP_ARROW** key as many times as you need to in order to bring up the function declaration and change it in *two places* (add a parameter in the parens and remove the line hardcoding the `customerAge`) so it looks like this:

```
function mayIOrderAKidsMeal(customerAge) {
    let maxAgeToOrderKidsMeal = 10;
    if (customerAge <= maxAgeToOrderKidsMeal) {
        console.log("You may order a kid's meal!");
    } else {
        console.log('Sorry.  You need to order from the adult menu.');
    }
}
```

Instead of hardcoding `customerAge` inside the function, it is now an parameter in the function that should be passed in as an argument when we call the function! Now try this:

```
// youngKidAge is called an "argument" because we're passing it in
mayIOrderAKidsMeal(youngKidAge);
```
Response: `"You may order a kid's meal!"` // Hooray!

```
mayIOrderAKidsMeal(48); // We have standards here
```
Response: `"Sorry.  You need to order from the adult menu."`

```
mayIOrderAKidsMeal(10); // Will it work for 10 year olds?
mayIOrderAKidsMeal(11); // C'mon, her birthday was just last week!
```

So that's hopefully a thorough enough explanation of `if`...`else` blocks to get you started. We'll be doing a lot more work with these and other conditionals in the rest of this book, so I hope you paid good attention. Now it's time to move on to a fun project we can do together that uses these principles! Close everything down, then open up an `about:blank` page with a console window in Chrome.

Follow Along: Minimum Height to Ride

The fair is in town! Hooray!

Oh wait…Look again…It's only for giraffes. :-(

Bummer! Well, maybe we can help out at least. The giraffe ferris wheel and bumper cars are open to anyone, but the giraffe tilt-a-whirl has a minimum height requirement of 102 inches tall. Your mission is to create a program that can accept the giraffe's height (in feet and inches, like 6'3") and respond with a message letting the giraffe know if he is tall enough to ride!

Sounds reasonable enough! Let's start by creating the function declaration with the parameters we expect to receive (include the `//TODO:` comment below):

```
function isGiraffeTallEnoughToRide(heightInFeet, additionalInches) {
    //TODO: add code here soon
}
```

Next, we need to convert our giraffe's height into just inches. We know that there are 12 inches in a foot, so let's first make that conversion (put all of these indented lines *inside* the function in place of the `//TODO:` comment):

```
    let numberOfInchesInAFoot = 12;
```

```
    let giraffeHeight = heightInFeet * numberOfInchesInAFoot;
```

And we also need to add the additional inches, which are passed in to our function:

```
    giraffeHeight += additionalInches; // remember what += does?
```

Now we use a comparison operator in an `if` statement to see if the giraffe is tall enough:

```
    let minimumHeight = 102;
    if (giraffeHeight >= minimumHeight) {
        console.log("You're tall enough to ride the tilt-a-whirl!");
    }
```

Let's also add an `else` block so that we'll have code that runs whenever the comparison operator condition resolves to `false`:

```
    } else {
        console.log("You're too short for this ride.  Try the ferris wheel.");
    }
```

So here's how the function should look all together:

```
function isGiraffeTallEnoughToRide(heightInFeet, additionalInches) {
    let numberOfInchesInAFoot = 12;
    let giraffeHeight = heightInFeet * numberOfInchesInAFoot;
    giraffeHeight += additionalInches;
    let minimumHeight = 102;
    if (giraffeHeight >= minimumHeight) {
        console.log("You're tall enough to ride the tilt-a-whirl!");
    } else {
        console.log("You're too short for this ride.  Try the ferris wheel.");
    }
}
```

With such a finely made function, we can now call it with each giraffe we need to test out!

Our lineup is in! The giraffes are 7'4" (that means 7 feet and 4 inches tall), 13'5" (13 ft. 5 in.), 10'9", 18'2", 6'11", 8'6", and 19'0". We can actually test them all out together with just one line at a time!

```
isGiraffeTallEnoughToRide(7, 4); // is 7 feet, 4 inches tall enough?
isGiraffeTallEnoughToRide(13, 5); //what about 13 ft, 5 in.?
isGiraffeTallEnoughToRide(10, 9); //10'9"
isGiraffeTallEnoughToRide(18, 2);
isGiraffeTallEnoughToRide(6, 11);
isGiraffeTallEnoughToRide(8, 6);
isGiraffeTallEnoughToRide(19, 0);
```

How did you do? If done perfectly, you should've found that only two of these seven giraffes were too short for the tilt-a-whirl (though one made it without an inch to spare!). Is that what you got?

And isn't it cool how you were able to make one nicely designed function and then call it as many times as you needed to in order to solve a

repeated problem? That is one of the most useful concepts in coding. Build a program once and then use it as many times as you like after that. Some programs are used thousands or even millions of times!

CHAPTER 5: **QUIZ**

Do the whole quiz in your Workbook without looking back at the chapter. After you're finished, check your answers against the back of the book.

1.   What is the name for the primitive data type that must always be one of two values: either `true` or `false`?

2.   What is the symbol for the comparison operator that checks if the value on the left side is smaller than the value on the right side?

3.   True/False: `"This one's tricky." !== 'This one\'s tricky.';`

4.   What is the preferred comparison operator for checking if two values are *not* equivalent?

5.   Which are the two comparison operators that I recommend you should *not* use in any of your own code?

6.   Which comparison operator checks if the value on the right is less than or equal to the value on the left?

7.   What general kind of statement in coding is used to perform certain blocks of code based on a given *condition*?

8.   If a value isn't an exact boolean data type (i.e., it's not either `true` or `false`), but when placed inside of the parens in an `if` block, it still causes that block of code to run, it can be said that this value is generally _____. If the `if` block would not be run based on this condition, then the value is said to be generally _____.

9.   What kind of statement is run only when the condition for an `if` block has resolved to `false`?

10.   True/False: Comparison operators always result in a value of `true` or `false`.

11.   True/False: Comparison operators are often used inside the parens of an `if` block.

12.   True/False: Comparison operators may sometimes be used inside the parens of an `else` statement.

13.   True/False: An `if/else` statement may only be used outside of a function.

CHAPTER 5: **KEY CONCEPTS**

Read this list and look back in the chapter to review anything you're not solid on before moving on:

- Boolean values
- All 8 Comparison Operators
- "Triple Equals" & "Not Equals Equals"
- "Greater Than" & "Less Than"
- "Greater Than or Equal To" & "Less Than or Equal To"
- Never Use "Double Equals" or "Not Equals"
- Conditionals
- `if` Statement
- Truthy & Falsy
- `if...else`

CHAPTER 5: **DRILLS**

A. Try typing these valid code snippets in the console

As you type the comparisons into the console, ask yourself if you expect the value to be **true** or **false**. Then look at the response from the console. If it's different from what you expected, see if you can determine why.

1.
```
'This string' === "This String";
```

2.
```
if (5 !== '5') {
    alert("didn't think so.");
}
```

3.
```
7 >= 7;
```

4.
```
9 <= 12;
```

5.
```
if ('abc' > 'ab') {
    console.log('truthy');
} else {
    console.log('falsy');
}
```

6.
```
0 !== false;
```

7.
```
if (false != 0) {
    console.log('easy peasy');
} else {
    console.log('kinda confusing');
}
```

```
8.    true == 5;

9.    if (1 == true) {
          alert('See why we don\'t use this?  Confusing!');
      } else {
          alert('I thought it was true!');
      }

10.   -7 > 0;

11.   4 < -20;

12.   true === 'true';

13.   if (1 === '1') {
          console.log('true dat');
      }

14.   // pay close attention to this one.  make sure you understand it!
      function whichNumberIsGreater(firstNumber, secondNumber) {
          if (firstNumber > secondNumber) {
              console.log(firstNumber + ' is greater than ' + secondNumber);
          } else {
              if (firstNumber < secondNumber) {
                  console.log(secondNumber + ' is greater than ' + firstNumber);
              } else {
                  console.log('Both numbers are equal!');
              }
          }
      }

15.   whichNumberIsGreater(212, 301);

16.   whichNumberIsGreater(155, -800);

17.   whichNumberIsGreater(12, 12);

18.   whichNumberIsGreater('abcd', 'efg');

19.   whichNumberIsGreater('24', 24);
```

B. What's wrong with each of these code snippets?

```
1.    function whichIsSmaller(numberA, numberB) {
          if (numberA < numberB) {
              console.log(a + ' is smaller!');
          } else {
              console.log(b + ' is smaller!');
          }
      }

2.    if {
          true;
      } else {
          false;
      }
```

3.
```
if (true) {
    console.log('truthy');
} else (false) {
    console.log('falsy');
}
```

4.
```
3 === 3 < 4;
```

5.
```
5 = 5;
```

6.
```
let numberValue === 5;
```

7.
```
let anotherNumber != 3;
```

CHAPTER 5: **AGGREGATE REVIEW**

1. True/False: Block comments cause the JavaScript interpreter to ignore everything from the start of the comment to the end of the current line.

2. Is this a valid statement? (And if not, why not?)
```
let isPizzaDelicious = 'Chef' !== 'Oscar the Grouch';
```

3. What characters can you *add* to this statement to avoid a Syntax Error?
```
let sadSong = "It's So Hard to Say "Goodbye" to Yesterday";
```

4. What does D.R.Y. stand for in coding?

5. What general kind of statement in coding is used to perform certain blocks of code based on a given *condition*?

6. Does this appear to accomplish the developer's intention? (And if not, why not?)
```
let daysPerWeek = 7; // used in calculations
```

7. Which data type is this?
```
'true'
```

8. What symbol(s) is/are used for block comments?

9. A value that isn't a boolean, but is treated as `false` for the purpose of conditional statements is said to be generally _____. If it were treated as `true` (though not a boolean), it is said to be generally _____.

10. What does the `%` operator indicate in JavaScript?

11. What form of capitalization should you use with function names in JavaScript?

12. True/False: An effective way to handle a string containing apostrophes is to use double quotes on the outside (surrounding the string).

13. What kind of error message would result from this code?
```
let firstInitial = 'J';
let firstInitial = "M";
```

14. What is a developer trying to arrive at when he/she uses modulo in an operation?

15. Is this a valid statement? (And if not, why not?)
```
(15 + (7 * 9) - 4) / 8 - 57);
```

16. True/False: Error messages are intended to obscure (hide) the cause of their errors in an attempt to stop hackers.

17. What does a single equals sign imply in a statement?

18. What keyboard shortcut is used for opening up the console in Chrome?

19. Is this valid code (feel free to type it in the console)? (And if not, why not?)
```
function isOldEnoughToEnlist(age) {
    let minimumAge = 18;
    if (age > minimumAge) {
        console.log('Old enough!');
    } else {
        console.log('Too young!');
    }
}
let myCurrentAge = 18;
isOldEnoughToEnlist(myCurrentAge);
```

20. What special symbol could you use to simplify this assignment?
```
greeting = greeting + ', ' + firstName;
```

21. Which data type is this?
```
false
```

22. Is this valid JavaScript? (And if not, why not?)
```
function returnANumber(startingNumber) {
    return startingNumber + 4;
    startingNumber += 3;
    console.log('New number: ' + startingNumber);
}
returnANumber(15);
```

23. What URL address should you go to in order to get an empty page in Chrome?

24. Chrome, Internet Explorer, Edge, Firefox, and Safari are all examples of _____.

25. Which two comparison operators should you avoid using in your own code?

26. Which comparison operator checks if the value on the right is greater than or equal to the value on the left?

27. What key should you press to indent your code inside a function?

28. Is this correct? (And if not, why not?)

```
let booleanCondition = true !== false;
if (booleanCondition) {
    console.log('It\'s truthy!');
} else {
    console.log("It's falsy!");
}
```

29. If you call a function inside of another function, the inner function is said to be _____ within the outer function.

30. True/False: Comparison operators always result in a boolean value.

31. What built-in function can you use to generate a random number between 0 and 1?

DIY: Children's Church

Pastor Preachit has just announced the grand opening of a new children's church, and it seems that everyone in the congregation wants to attend—including the adults and the babies! Of course there isn't enough space for everybody, so it's important to the Pastor that the children's church is limited exclusively to children between the ages of 6 and 13.

Build a function that can help Pastor Preachit by accepting a person's age (as an argument), then logging a message to the console stating whether or not that person meets the minimum *and* maximum age requirements to attend children's church.

Try passing in many different ages to make sure your function works in the console. After you're done with this project (or before you're done if you're struggling with it), check to see how your answer compares with the one in the back of the book.

LOGICALLY OPERATIONAL

If you were able to follow and understand all of the last chapter, then this one should be a breeze! In the last chapter, we introduced the third of the five different primitive data types, and in this chapter, you'll learn the last two. And guess what! They're the easiest ones of all!

Null

The fourth primitive data type is a simple one: **null**. Null basically means *nothing*. Is it `0`? No, zero is a number. Is it `""`? No, that's an empty string. Is it `false`? No, `false` is a boolean. So which is it? It's `null`. Nothing. The fourth data type. Here's an example of how you might use it:

```
let myVariable = null;
myVariable;
```
Response: `null`

This is a useful way of setting a value on something that is intended to be changed sometime in the future. By setting it to a `null` value, you're kind of making a statement that this variable will need to be changed in the future or ignored.

As an example, suppose you'd like to create a form for a user to fill out. The form has three fields in it: `name`, `age`, and `carColor`. In creating the form, you might need to set some initial values for each of these variables. You might set the initial values like this:

```
let name = null;
let age = null;
let carColor = null;
```

After the user fills out the form, you'll have values that can be used for these:

```
name = 'Kaori';
age = 13;
```

But wait! Kaori is too young to drive a car, so she has no `carColor`! No problem. We'll keep that value as `null` (because Kaori didn't fill in that field). Now when we're processing the form (we'll show how to do that in the next volume when we talk about forms), we'll know to ignore the `carColor` field, which has the value of `null`.

Another thing to note about `null` is that it is *falsy*. Do you remember what that means? If not, look it up in the glossary! Don't be lazy! Type this in the console to see what I mean:

```
let testCondition = null;
if (testCondition) {
    console.log('Looks like ' + testCondition + ' is truthy after all! '
        + 'I guess Jeremy doesn\'t know what he\'s talking about!');
} else {
    console.log(testCondition + ' is indeed falsy. '
        + 'I never should have doubted such a brilliant author.');
}
```

So this primitive data type is quite simple. The null data type has exactly one possible value: `null`. It will become more useful in the future when we learn about JavaScript objects because, in some ways, `null` is considered to be the simplest of all objects.

Ya know what? That's confusing. Forget that last part; I'm getting ahead of myself.

You've now learned four of the five primitive data types. Let's finish out the list, shall we?

Undefined

The fifth—and final—primitive data type is...`undefined`!

Whoa!! What a plot twist! The final data type is one you've been seeing in this book ever since Chapter 1!

As a data type, **undefined** means that no other value has been assigned to a variable, not even `null`. This is the default value for a variable. Type this in your console for example:

```
let myCoolNewVariable;
myCoolNewVariable;
```

This is probably the first time we've used the `let` keyword in a line that did *not* have an = sign. That's because if we want the value `undefined`, we simply don't have to assign any other value. The variable receives the value `undefined` by default!

Finally, what would you guess would happen if we put `undefined` in a conditional statement? Do you think it would resolve truthy or falsy? Let's try it in the console to see:

```
let newUndefinedVariable;
if (newUndefinedVariable) {
    console.log(newUndefinedVariable + ' is truthy! ' + 'Just as I suspected!');
} else {
    console.log('I knew it! ' + newUndefinedVariable + ' is falsy!');
}
```

Was that what you expected? I hope so!

Well now you've learned all five of the primitive data types in JavaScript! You'll get many opportunities to use all five of them throughout this book. But for now, let's move on to some new useful tools for your JavaScript toolbox!

Logical Operators

In the last chapter, you learned about comparison operators such as `<`, `>=`, `===`, and `!==`. In this chapter, I'll introduce you to some of their close relatives called **logical operators**.

There are three logical operators: `&&`, `||`, and `!`. Similar to the comparison operators, the logical operators are often used with boolean values. They can also be used with other data types (such as strings and numbers). Unlike comparison operators, their results are not always boolean (`true` or `false`), but as with *all* possible values, they are still always truthy or falsy (which means they can be treated like they're `true` or `false`). For this reason, they work great in conditional statements like `if...else`.

Gosh, that last paragraph went through several rewrites, and it still sounds confusing! I think we'd better look at a few examples to show you what I mean.

Logical AND (`&&`)

The first logical operator is represented by the ampersand symbol (`&` —which is located above the 7 key on your keyboard) *doubled*, so it looks like this: `&&`. We refer to this as "**logical AND**" (though I think most developers just say "and and"). This is used to determine if two different values are *both* truthy.

Before we try this out, let's think through a real-life scenario that could use the logical AND (`&&`). Suppose your mom wants to know if you're ready for school. She says, "To be ready for school, you need your backpack AND your lunch. Are you ready for school?"

"Mom, what if I have neither my backpack nor my lunch?"
"Um... you're not ready (obvi)."
"Okay, I have my backpack, just not my lunch. We good?"
"Nope!"
"Alright, I went back to get my lunch and left my backpack on the counter."
(Facepalm)
"Mom! I've got my backpack AND my lunch!"
"Yes! You're [finally] ready for school!"

Notice that only in the last scenario was the result a passing one (i.e., "truthy"). It was falsy in all the other cases.

Close down all the programs on your computer, then open up a blank console window in Chrome. Type out these examples, and pay close attention to the results (see if you can guess what the console response will be for each!):

```
false && false;
true && true;
true && false;
false && true;
```

The result of the second line is `true` because the values on *both* sides of the `&&` are truthy. All the other three lines have at least one falsy value, so you can't say that *both* sides are truthy. Get it?

Another way of saying it is that `&&` will return *falsy* if the value on *either* side is falsy. This might sound strange at first, but if you look at the example above, you'll see that's correct.

Let's try this out in the console using a function. Also, I just remembered that your teacher explicitly told me you *must* start wearing shoes to school. (Hey, I don't make the rules around here!) So let's add that one more parameter:

```
function amIReadyForSchool(haveBackpack, haveLunch, haveShoes) {
    if (haveBackpack && haveLunch && haveShoes) {
        console.log('You\'re ready for school!');
    } else {
        console.log("You're not ready yet!  Hurry or we'll be late!");
    }
}

/* the order of the values (called "arguments") corresponds to
 * the parameters in the function definition above.
 * i.e. the first boolean stands for haveBackpack, the second for haveLunch, etc.
 *
 * BTW, when writing comments, you don't need to type every word I have here
 * Just a couple words is fine to get the idea
 */
amIReadyForSchool(false, false, true);
amIReadyForSchool(true, false, true);
// leaving out an argument is the same as passing in undefined for that argument
amIReadyForSchool(true, true);
amIReadyForSchool(true, true, true);
```

Logical OR (||)

The second logical operator is represented by the pipe symbol (| —which is located above the BACKSLASH key on your keyboard) *doubled*, so it looks like this: ||. We refer to this as "**logical OR**" (though I think most developers just say "or or"). This is used to determine if *either* of two different values are truthy. Let's use a basic example again:

```
false || false;
true || true;
```

```
true || false;
false || true;
```

The result of the first line is `false` because *neither* of the values on *either* side of the || are truthy. All the other three lines have at least one truthy value, so you can correctly say that *at least one* of the two sides is truthy. Get it?

Another way of saying it is that || will only return *falsy* if *both* sides are falsy. This might sound strange at first, but if you look at the example above, you'll see that's correct.

Here's a simple real-life scenario that could use the logical OR (||). Before leaving for school, your mom says you have to eat breakfast. You can eat eggs or cereal (or both). But you must eat something; it's the most important meal of the day! So, have you eaten breakfast? Type this out in the console:

```
function isBreakfastEaten(ateEggs, ateCereal) {
    if (ateEggs || ateCereal) {
        console.log("You've eaten breakfast!");
    } else {
        console.log('You have not eaten breakfast
yet!  Hop to it');
    }
}
```

Remember, you can use the **UP_ARROW** key to bring up previous lines of code. Can you guess the results of each line here?

```
isBreakfastEaten(false, true);
isBreakfastEaten(true, true);
isBreakfastEaten(true, false);
isBreakfastEaten(false, false);
```

Do you see the difference between && and ||?

Now, let's try putting them together. If you want to leave the house in the morning, you should know by now all the requirements your mom has for you. In order to leave the house, you must eat breakfast (*either* eggs OR cereal) AND have your backpack AND lunch AND shoes.

Can you figure out how to make a single function for all of your requirements? If so, do it now in the console before reading further. If you don't think you can do it yet, then read on and type along with me, but try to see how much of it you can come up with on your own. Either way, you must type it all into the console.

```
function canWeLeaveNow(ateEggs, ateCereal, haveBackpack, haveLunch, haveShoes) {
    if ((ateEggs || ateCereal) && (haveBackpack && haveLunch && haveShoes)) {
        console.log('We can leave!  Great job!');
    } else {
        console.log("Not yet!  You're not ready!");
    }
}
```

Now try to guess what the result will be for each of these:

```
canWeLeaveNow(false, true, true, true, false);
canWeLeaveNow(true, true, false, true, true);
canWeLeaveNow(true, false, true, true, true);
// leaving out an argument is the same as passing in undefined (which is falsy)
canWeLeaveNow(true, true, true, true);
canWeLeaveNow(false, true, true, true, true);
```

Make sense? Great!

Always Truthy/Falsy... Not Always True/False

In looking at the provided examples, you may have asked yourself "Why does he keep writing 'truthy' and 'falsy'? Why not just write 'true' and 'false'?" Or maybe that thought never crossed your mind. Either way, I'll answer that for you now.

In the case of both `&&` and `||`, the value returned will not always be `true` or `false`. It will actually be one of the values on one of the two sides of the logical operator! Try these (you don't need to type the comments unless you want to):

```
true && 5;
0 && 5; // 0 is falsy, so the 5 is ignored
'hi' && undefined && true; // returns the first falsy value (ignores the rest)
true && 1 && null && 'good';
true && 'good' && 'honest' && 'noble'; // no falsy values, so returns last value

true || 5; // returns the first truthy value (ignores the rest);
0 || 5;
'loyal' || 'kind' && 'honest' || false; // returns the first truthy value
false || 0 || undefined || "" || null; // no truthy values, so returns last value
```

So the values that are returned aren't always booleans. But because all values are either truthy or falsy, this still works fine as a substitute for the *actual* booleans (`true` and `false`).

Okay, I hope that helped to clear up that question you probably weren't asking. Now let's move on to the last logical operator!

Logical NOT (!)

The third and final logical operator is represented by the exclamation point symbol (`!` —which is achieved with the **SHIFT+1** key combination on your keyboard). We refer to this as "**logical NOT**" (though most developers just say "not" or sometimes "bang"). Try it out:

```
!true; // false
!false; // true
```

Logical NOT is downright *contrarian*! This means that it's almost like whatever you give him, he says the opposite! You say, "Isn't this a beautiful, warm, sunny day?" and logical NOT will probably say, "No, it's an ugly, cold, rainy night,"...or more accurately, its closest boolean equivalent: `false`.

One interesting thing to note is that, unlike logical AND and logical OR, logical NOT *always* returns a boolean (either `true` or `false`). Try typing these examples and notice the results:

```
!0; // true (because 0 is a falsy value, ! makes it boolean true)
!5; // false (because 5 is truthy)
!(100 > 1);
!(5 !== 5);
!'string of any length';
!""; // empty string (use double or single quotes)
!(true && true);
!(false || false);
!!true; // two !'s (pronounced "not not")
!!0; // this is the same as !(!0);
```

Let's try using logical NOT in a function. The first thing we'll need to...Oh, hold on...that's my cell phone...I better take this. I'll be right back...

Okay, I'm back. That was your teacher. Turns out the school is concerned about sickness—specifically fevers and throwing up. The new rule is that a student should NOT come to school if she has a temperature of MORE THAN 100 degrees OR if she has puked all over herself. It's embarrassing to have to put that right here in my book, but...teacher's orders. Can you think of a formula (using logical NOT) for determining if you're healthy enough to go to school? If you can write it on your own, do it; otherwise try this one:

```
function amIHealthyEnough(myTemperature, havePukedAllOverMyself) {
    let maxHealthyTemperature = 100;
    if (!(myTemperature > maxHealthyTemperature || havePukedAllOverMyself)) {
        console.log("You're healthy enough for school!");
    } else {
        console.log("Go back to bed!  You're too sick for school!");
    }
}
```

Notice that the first parameter expects a number and the second parameter expects a boolean. Let's invoke this function together with different arguments:

```
amIHealthyEnough(100, false);
amIHealthyEnough(99.8, true); // yuck... who's gonna clean this up?
amIHealthyEnough(150, false); // hmm... let me see that thermometer...
amIHealthyEnough(98.6, false); // Thought so!  Probably just a math test.
```

Okay! Now let's go ahead and add all these together. You may have guessed that this example is a little more convoluted, or complicated, than you would likely have in a real program. You'll learn a better way to organize this stuff in a later volume when we talk about *refactoring*. In the meantime though, let's just tack on the new stuff to our old function. If it's still in the console history from before, you can bring it up again by click the **UP_ARROW** key several times. Then change it as follows:

```
function canWeLeaveNow(myTemperature, havePukedAllOverMyself, ateEggs, ateCereal,
haveBackpack, haveLunch, haveShoes) {
    let maxHealthyTemperature = 100;
    if (!(myTemperature > maxHealthyTemperature || havePukedAllOverMyself)
        && (ateEggs || ateCereal)
        && (haveBackpack && haveLunch && haveShoes)) {
        console.log('Hooraaayyyy!  We can leave for school!  Great job!');
    } else {
        console.log("No way, Jose!  You're either too sick or not ready!");
    }
}

/**
 * Pay special attention to the order of the values being passed in ("arguments").
 * Each argument corresponds with the parameters in the function declaration above.
 */
canWeLeaveNow(97.9, false, false, true, true, true, true);
canWeLeaveNow(101, false, true, false, true, true, true);
canWeLeaveNow(98.6, true, true, true, true, true, true);
canWeLeaveNow(98.6, false, true, true, false, true, true);
canWeLeaveNow(100, false, true, false, true, true, true);
```

Phew! That was a big one! Now on to one more new concept. If you understood the stuff before, this next one should be a breeze.

if...else if...else

By now, you probably feel like an `if...else` expert! Well, I'm afraid that's only partly true. One thing every `if...else` expert needs to learn is `else if`!

Suppose you just got a new alarm clock for your birthday. You'd like to write a program to wake you up on time. On school days (Monday–Friday), you need to wake up by 6:30 to get to school on time. But on Saturdays, you can sleep in as long as you like! Here's how you can write your function:

```
function timeToWakeUp(dayOfTheWeek) {
    if (dayOfTheWeek === 'Saturday') {
        return null; // no alarm today
    } else {
        return '6:30';
    }
}
timeToWakeUp('Tuesday');
timeToWakeUp('Saturday');
```

That works great! Oh, but wait...on Sundays, you need a 7:30 alarm to get to church on time. So now there are *three* possibilities. This looks like a job for `else if`! Press the **UP_ARROW** a few times to get your function back and change it like so:

```
function timeToWakeUp(dayOfTheWeek) {
    if (dayOfTheWeek === 'Saturday') {
        return null; // no alarm today
    } else if (dayOfTheWeek === 'Sunday') {
```

```
        return '7:30';
    } else {
        return '6:30';
    }
}
timeToWakeUp('Sunday');
timeToWakeUp('Friday');
timeToWakeUp('Saturday');
```

So you see that if we use `else if`, we also need to put another conditional statement inside the parens after that second `if` (the one that immediately follows `else`). If this statement is truthy, we'll run the code in that `if` block, `else` we run the code in the `else` block below it.

Hey, I just thought of something! Let's use the new `else if` knowledge we've just acquired to make our `canWeLeaveNow` function even more helpful by giving more meaningful error messages! Let's retype the whole thing with many changes to incorporate what we've learned! Remember to use **SHIFT+ENTER** for break returns. Type along with me:

```
function canWeLeaveNow(myTemperature, havePukedAllOverMyself, ateEggs, ateCereal,
haveBackpack, haveLunch, haveShoes) {
    let maxHealthyTemperature = 100;
    let message; // undefined (for now);

    if (myTemperature > maxHealthyTemperature) {
        message = "You're running a fever.  You should be in bed today.";
    } else if (havePukedAllOverMyself) {
        message = 'You really want to go to school with puke on your shirt? '
            + 'Get in the bath.';
    } else {
        if (ateEggs || ateCereal) {
            if (!haveBackpack) {
                message = 'Get your backpack!';
            } else if (!haveLunch) {
                message = 'Get your lunch!';
            } else if (!haveShoes) {
                message = 'Get your shoes!';
            } else {
                message = 'We can leave for school!  Great job!';
            }
        } else {
            message = 'You need breakfast--the most important meal of the day!";
        }
    }

    console.log(message);
}
```

Now I recognize that this function is huge. It's the biggest one we've created so far in this book. But it's also very logical, and in some ways it should be more readable than the smaller version we made before. We're now going to invoke the function several times with different arguments. For each of these lines, I'd like you to mentally walk through the function and see if you can guess what the exact response will be before you press **ENTER**.

```
canWeLeaveNow(99.1, false, true, true, false, true, true);
canWeLeaveNow(102, false, true, false, true, false, true);
canWeLeaveNow(98.1, false, true, true, true, true, true);
```

```
canWeLeaveNow(98.6, true, true, true, true, true, true);
canWeLeaveNow(99.9, false, true, false, true, false, true);
canWeLeaveNow(98.6, false, false, false, true, true, true);
canWeLeaveNow(100.0, false, false, true, true, true, true);
```

Alrighty! How did you do with that?! Do you feel that you understood it all? If not, please go back and try this chapter again from the beginning one more time before moving on. Trust me, you'll be able to move much faster the second time through it. Also, if you come across words that you've forgotten, try looking them up in the glossary. Remember, the purpose of reading this book is not so you can get through it and complete a book report. The important thing is to understand and *retain* the knowledge. You can do it!

Follow Along: Movie Tickets

Your local movie theater needs your help! They need a program that will determine for them if a child is old enough to watch any given movie. The movies that are playing now are rated G, PG-13, and R. At this theater, moviegoers of all ages are allowed to watch the G-rated movies; anyone over the age of 10 may watch the PG-13 movies; but R-rated movies are restricted to patrons who are at least 17 years old. What kind of function can we write to determine if the customer may buy a ticket?

If you think you know how to solve this (or at least how to get started), I would encourage you to try it out on your own before moving on. If you're not sure where to begin, then by all means, do some of this along with me. But first, please close down all programs, then reopen the blank Chrome page with a console. Ready? Okay:

```
function isAllowedToWatchTheMovie(movieRating, customerAge) {
    let minAgeForR = 17;
    let minAgeForPg13 = 10;
    let msg = null; // "msg" is a common shorthand for "message"

    if (movieRating === 'R' && customerAge >= minAgeForR) {
        msg = 'You may watch this R-rated film.';
    } else if (movieRating === 'PG-13' && !(customerAge < minAgeForPg13)) {
        msg = 'You may watch this PG-13-rated film.';
    } else if (movieRating === 'G') {
        msg = 'Anyone may watch this G-rated film.';
    } else {
        msg = 'Sorry, you are not allowed to watch.';
    }

    console.log(msg);
}
```

To make sure this works, try out different combinations of arguments on your own such as:

```
isAllowedToWatchTheMovie('PG-13', 10);
isAllowedToWatchTheMovie('R', 15);
isAllowedToWatchTheMovie('G', 7);
isAllowedToWatchTheMovie('R', 17);
```

Did that work for you? Great! Once again, the day is saved, thanks to...What's that? Oh! Okay... turns out, the movie theater has got some complaints for us. Apparently, the rules state that the age restrictions do *not* apply for any patrons who are here with their parents. So the rule is that kids can enter any movies as long as they're accompanied by an adult. Okay so that shouldn't be too hard, right? Go ahead and bring up your function definition and let's make a few alterations to it (remember, there's more than one way to do this; also, if you can make these changes on your own without looking, that's even better!):

```
function isAllowedToWatchTheMovie(movieRating, customerAge, withAdult) {
    let minAgeForR = 17;
    let minAgeForPg13 = 10;
    let msg = null; // "msg" is a common shorthand for "message"

    if (movieRating === 'R' && (customerAge >= minAgeForR || withAdult)) {
        msg = 'You may watch this R-rated film.';
    } else if (movieRating === 'PG-13'
            && (!(customerAge < minAgeForPg13) || withAdult)) {
        msg = 'You may watch this PG-13-rated film.';
    } else if (movieRating === 'G') {
        msg = 'Anyone may watch this G-rated film.';
    } else {
        msg = 'Sorry, you are not allowed to watch.';
    }

    console.log(msg);
}

isAllowedToWatchTheMovie('PG-13', 9, false);
isAllowedToWatchTheMovie('PG-13', 9, true);
isAllowedToWatchTheMovie('G', 7); // leaving an argument out = undefined
isAllowedToWatchTheMovie('R', 16);
isAllowedToWatchTheMovie('R', 15, true);
```

And just like that, you're the town hero once again! All in a day's work. Whoosh!

CHAPTER 6: **QUIZ**

Do the whole quiz in your Workbook without looking back at the chapter. After you're finished, have a parent check your answers against the back of the book (or check them yourself if no parent is available).

1.   What is the name for the primitive data type that means no other value has been assigned?

2.   Similar to the comparison operators, the _____ operators (`&&`, `||`, and `!`) work great in conditional statements.

3.   What is the name for the primitive data type that basically means *nothing* (not zero, not empty string, not `undefined`, not `false`, etc.)?

4.   If a function definition has four parameters, but only two arguments are passed in, what are the values that the third and fourth parameters receive?

5.   What is the name for the logical operator that will only return falsy if it has falsy values on *both* sides? What is the symbol for this logical operator?

6.   How many possible values are there for the null data type?

7.   True/False: `53 >= 53 && !(51 <= 52);`

8.   If the condition inside the parens of an `if` block returns falsy, what syntax might you use to check a different condition before resolving to the `else` block?

9.   What is the name for the *only* logical operator that *always* returns a boolean? What is the symbol for this logical operator?

10.   True/False: Any/Every value in JavaScript can either be considered truthy or falsy?

11.   What is the name for the logical operator that will return truthy if it has a truthy value on *either* side? What is the symbol for this logical operator?

12.   True/False: `true || false;`

13.   True/False: `false || (true && false);`

14.   True/False: `null and undefined are both falsy values.`

15.   What is the name for the logical operator that will return falsy if it has a falsy value on *either* side? What is the symbol for this logical operator?

16.   True/False: `null || false !== undefined;`

17.   What is the value of `myMessage` after this line?
        `let myMessage;`

18. How many possible values are there for the undefined data type?

19. True/False: `(null || false) || ((0 || true) || undefined);`

20. What is the value of `imFeeling` after this line?
    ```
    var imFeeling = !'sure' || !!'confused';
    ```

21. What is the name for the logical operator that will only return truthy if it has truthy values on *both* sides? What is the symbol for this logical operator?

22. The values `null`, `false`, `''`, `0`, and `undefined` are all _____; whereas `true`, `'string'`, and `1` are all _____ values.

23. What's the value of `theGreatestOfThese` after this line?
    ```
    var theGreatestOfThese = 'faith' && 'hope' && 'love';
    ```

CHAPTER 6: **KEY CONCEPTS**

Read this list and look back in the chapter to review anything you're not solid on before moving on:

- Null data type with its one possible value: `null`
- Undefined data type with its one possible value: `undefined`
- All 3 Logical Operators
- Logical AND (`&&`)
- Logical OR (`||`)
- Logical NOT (`!`)
- Different return values of `&&`, `||` and `!`
- `if...else if...else`

CHAPTER 6: **DRILLS**

A. Try typing these valid code snippets in the console

As you type the comparisons into the console, ask yourself what exactly you expect the value to be. Then look at the response from the console to see if you're correct.

1. ```
   true && false && true;
   ```

2. ```
   true || false || true;
   ```

3. ```
   if (5 < 4) {
       console.log('A');
   } else if (5 > 4) {
       console.log('B');
   ```
   ```

```
  } else {
      console.log('C');
  }
```

4.
```
3 && (null || ((15 / 3) - 5));
```

5.
```
if ('abc' > 'd') {
    console.log('A');
} else if (0) {
    console.log('B');
} else {
    console.log('C');
}
```

6.
```
if (5 && 'dime' && null) {
    console.log('A');
} else if (0 || undefined || '') {
    console.log('B');
} else if (false || -1 || !0) {
    console.log('C');
} else {
    console.log('D');
}
```

7.
```
// pay close attention to this one.  make sure you understand it!
function eldersFirst(person1Age, person2Age) {
    let whoseTurn;
    if ((!person2Age && person1Age) || person1Age > person2Age) {
        whoseTurn = 1;
    } else if ((!person1Age && person2Age) || person2Age > person1Age) {
        whoseTurn = 2;
    } else {
        whoseTurn = null;
    }
    if (whoseTurn) {
        console.log('Person' + whoseTurn + ' is older and goes first.');
    } else if (!(person1Age || person2Age)) {
        console.log('No ages have been passed as arguments!');
    } else {
        console.log("Both are the same age. Let's randomly decide Person"
            + (Math.floor(Math.random() * 2) + 1) + ' goes first!');
    }
}
```

8.
```
eldersFirst(80, 10);
```

9.
```
eldersFirst(15, 17);
```

10.
```
eldersFirst(20);
```

11.
```
eldersFirst(null, null);
```

12.
```
eldersFirst(13, 13);
```

13.
```
eldersFirst();
```

14.
```
eldersFirst(null, 5);
```

```
15.    eldersFirst(7, 7);

16.    function unknownMan(nameTag) {
           console.log('His name is ' + (nameTag || 'John Doe') + '.');
       }

17.    unknownMan('Justin Thyme');

18.    unknownMan();

19.    unknownMan('Rusty Karr');

20.    unknownMan(null);
```

B. What's wrong with each of these code snippets?

```
1.    function notNot(anyArgument) {
          if (!!anyArgument) {
              console.log('anyArgument value is falsy');
          } else if (!anyArgument) {
              console.log('anyArgument value is falsy');
          } else {
              console.log('anyArgument value is truthy');
          }
      }

2.    if (25 > 14) {
          'Yes';
      } else if {
          'no';
      }

3.    let !yourHearts = 'be troubled';

4.    true && false = false;

5.    let x || 5 = !true;
```

CHAPTER 6: AGGREGATE REVIEW

1.   Is this a valid statement? (And if not, why not?)
```
let isMamasCookingTheBestInTown = !!'you bet it is!';
```

2.   What are the data types (in order) for each of these falsy values?
```
false; ""; null; 0; ''; undefined;
```

3.   What does the `%` operator indicate in JavaScript?

4.   A JavaScript string is made up of individual _____.

5.   True/False: Single-line comments cause the JavaScript interpreter to ignore everything from the start of the comment to the end of the current line.

6. There are three different _____ operators (`&&`, `||`, and `!`).

7. The _____ operators we use are `===`, `!==`, `>`, `>=`, `<`, and `<=`.

8. What general kind of statement in coding is used to perform certain blocks of code based on a given *condition*?

9. If you call a function inside of another function, the inner function is said to be _____ within the outer function.

10. Is this valid code (feel free to type it in the console)? (And if not, why not?)
```
function isAcceptableHeightForKidsPlayArea(height) {
    let minHeight = 24; // inches
    let maxHeight = 48;
    let verdict;
    if (height > minHeight && height < maxHeight) {
        verdict = 'Acceptable Height!';
    } else if (height > maxHeight) {
        verdict = 'Too tall!';
    } else {
        verdict = 'Too short!';
    }
    console.log(verdict);
}
isAcceptableHeightForKidsPlayArea(21);
isAcceptableHeightForKidsPlayArea(35);
isAcceptableHeightForKidsPlayArea(53);
isAcceptableHeightForKidsPlayArea(48);
```

11. True/False: Logical operators always result in a boolean value.

12. What special symbol could you use to simplify this assignment?
```
currentScore = currentScore + 10;
```

13. Which mathematical operator would be most useful for checking if a given value is evenly divisible by 52?

14. Which of these values are truthy? And what are the data types (in order) for each of the values?
```
" "; -1; true; 15.3; 'false'; '0';
```

15. Is this valid JavaScript? (And if not, why not?)
```
function tellMeHello(myName) {
    return myName + '!';
    console.log('Hello, ' + myName);
}
tellMeHello('Jeremy');
```

16. Which comparison operator returns `false` if the value on the left is greater than or equal to the value on the left?

17. Where can a developer type simple JavaScript commands to test them out and get immediate responses?

18. What day comes after Tuesday?

19. What key should you press to indent your code inside a function?

20. True/False: When there are multiple parens nested inside of one another, you should always evaluate the statements *from the outside in* (i.e. process the results of the values for the outer parens before processing those for the inner parens).

21. True/False: Comparison operators always result in a boolean value.

22. Is this valid JavaScript? (And if not, why not?)
```
function gimmeFive(5) {
    return 5;
}
gimmeFive(5);
```

23. What built-in function can you use to round a float (number with a decimal point) down to the nearest integer (number without a decimal point)?

24. True/False: `31 >= -31 && !(38 <= 38) || !!(-39 < 39);`

25. True/False: Code that is in comments is ignored by the JavaScript interpreter.

26. What key combination can you press to get a break return (new line) in the console?

DIY: Adventures of Lunk

A new adventure game is being released soon: *The Legend of Zebra: Wildly Bad Breath!* The game designers are almost ready to put it in production, but they're struggling to work out a bug in the logic of the final temple: the Temple of Stripes. Here's how they need the Temple Door to behave:

- If Lunk is missing any of the <u>6 Bi-Force pieces</u>, the templeDoor should send him away with a message telling him to get the rest of the pieces.
- If he has all the Bi-Force pieces, then he must show that he possesses *both* the halitosisWand *and* the masterKey (*or* 10 regularKeys if he doesn't have the masterKey).
- If he possesses the required wand *and* key(s), display a message congratulating him and letting him enter the Temple of Stripes.
- If he is missing the required wand and/or key(s), send him away with a cryptic, mostly unhelpful message saying to come back when he's more prepared. (The only way Lunk will learn what he still needs is if he randomly happens to bring onion stew to the mageSquire in obscureTown...Good luck with that.)

Build a single function—using `if...else if...else` blocks—that can properly work out this logic by accepting the required inventory items (as individual arguments like `hasMasterKey`, etc.) and using logical operators on them. Then try running the function with different arguments to ensure that it logs the appropriate message to the console for each scenario. (Note: the mageSquire stuff is *not* part of the solution; that's just to be silly.)

After you're done with this project (or before you're done if you're struggling with it), check to see how your answer compares with the one in the back of the book. Remember, there are several ways to get a correct answer. It just needs to work with all of the different possible inventory combinations that Lunk may have.

7 PROJECTS GALORE

Congratulations on getting this far! I hope you can appreciate how much you've learned in the last six chapters. It's quite extraordinary!

Well I think you'll find this chapter to be the most fun chapter we've done so far. You'll learn a few new small things, but mostly you'll get to exercise what you've learned already. This is your chance to flex your muscles and try out the concepts you've been learning on many different projects!

The format for this chapter is simple: I'll teach a small concept, then we'll do a project together. Then you'll do one by yourself. Then I'll teach another small concept, and we'll do another project together and you'll do one by yourself, etc. My challenge to you is to keep using your brain! By that, I mean don't check out on me and start just typing along to get through each project. I want you to really think through the projects and try to see if you can guess how to solve each one (maybe even try it yourself) before using the answer I give you. That's a major part of the job of a real developer (all that...ya know, like...thinking and stuff), and the more you can do that now, the better you will be!

Now before moving on, please close down every program on your computer, so you just see the desktop. Then open the blank page in Chrome (as we've done since Chapter 1) and open the Chrome developer tools console. Once you've done that, let's start with learning an important, fundamental JavaScript concept; then we can move on to the easier ones.

Methods in the Madness

For some of these projects, you will use these cool things called properties and methods. Here's a simple example of a property:

```
'abcdefg'.length;  // .length = how many characters are in this string?
Response: 7
```

When you see that tiny little dot (the period) between the string and the word following it, that tells you that the next word represents a property. A **property** is a named value that is attached to an object. What is an object? Hmm...ya had to ask, didn't you?

Okay...well...The following paragraph will probably sound confusing. It would take me a few pages to explain this concept fully, but I'm going to try to cram it into one paragraph because I don't want to divert our attention away from the projects, which are the main point of this chapter. I'll just put it this way: objects are a crucial part of JavaScript. JavaScript is full of objects. An **object** in JavaScript is a collection of properties (which are named values). Remember `Math.random()`? `Math` is an object and that dot (`.`) tells us that the next word `random` is a property. And because `random` is followed by parens (`()`), that tells us `random` must be a function (all functions have parens). When a property is a function, there's a special name for it: we call it a **method**.

Anyway, we're getting ahead of ourselves. You'll learn all about objects later. For now, just know that a string is one kind of object, so it has properties like `length` that will tell you stuff about it.

Objects also have *methods* (attached functions), which allow you to do stuff with them. When working with strings, a couple examples are the `.concat()` and `.repeat()` methods:

```
'The sky'.concat(' is blue.');   // behaves like using the + to concatenate
'Why? '.repeat(50);   // can you guess what this will do?  Test it out!
```

Now you can annoy your friends with a simple little line of code! You'll learn a bunch more new and useful properties and methods soon enough.

Phew! Sorry to get off on a long tangent like that. I have a hard time passing up those teachable moments sometimes—especially when it's something important to JavaScript like understanding objects, properties, and methods. But there's a process for learning effectively, and I really should get back to it. Now, where was I?

Oh yes! We're about to learn a couple new methods to prepare for our first project!

Changing Cases: `toUpperCase()` and `toLowerCase()`

We get to START with an EASY one! Have YOU ever NOTICED how some MESSAGES appear with TOO MUCH CAPITALIZATION? Doesn't it sometimes seem like people are SHOUTING at YOU when they CAPITALIZE EACH WORD?! Have you EVER WONDERED if you could CALM DOWN those people who LOVE THAT CAPS_LOCK KEY? Well...now you can.

You can take any string and return a new version of it in all capital letters by using the built-in string method `.toUpperCase()`. Similarly, you can return a new version of any string with all lower case letters with the built-in `.toLowerCase()` method. Remember, a method is simply a function attached to an object—in this case, a string. They work like this:

```
'I like pizza!'.toUpperCase();
"SERIOUSLY, STOP SHOUTING SO MUCH.".toLowerCase();

let nameOfUser = 'Frank';
let greeting = "It's so good to see you again, " + nameOfUser + '!';
console.log(greeting.toUpperCase() + ' I missed you so much!');
```

Any questions? No? Okay, let's do a project!

Follow Along: Shout Muffler

One of City Hall's most prominent financial
donors, Grum P. Oldman, gets anxious when
he reads shouted messages in the town's online
forum. It's important to keep him content,
so we'd like to install a shout muffler on his
machine. Whenever someone posts a message in
the forum, we'd like it to be converted to lowercase
letters. This will muffle the sound of people shouting to help Mr. Oldman remain calm. (...You're
right, this doesn't actually make much sense; just play along, okay?)

```
function shoutMuffler(message) {
    return message.toLowerCase();
}
// test it out
shoutMuffler("HERE'S AN OBNOXIOUS MESSAGE WRITTEN IN ALL CAPS!!");
shoutMuffler("emAil-AddrESSes@uSUAlly-wOrK-wiTH-anY-capITalizaTIOn.cOM");
```

Simple, right? Now try a project on your own!

DIY: Spam Email Formatter

You've been hired to help out a spam email distributor who works in the remote country of
Farawaynia. He has strict quality standards for his spam emails involving large sums of money,
required spelling and grammatical errors, a strong sense of urgency, and most of all: capitalization
of every letter. Most of these requirements have been outsourced to other developers (so you don't
need to worry about them). But the one thing you must do yourself is write a function that will
convert all messages to be fully capitalized.

Creating Variables with const

Alright now, this is one of the most important concepts of this chapter, so please pay close
attention. Remember how in chapter 1, I showed you how you could create a new variable using
the var keyword? Then remember how I told you that we would usually be using let instead of var
even though they do almost exactly the same thing (but I annoyingly did *not* tell you what actually
made them different)? Remember that time? Yeah...good times.

Well now you get to learn a *new* keyword that you can use to create variables...since you were always
itching to learn a *third* way to accomplish the same simple task! It's the const keyword (short for
"constant" which means an unchangeable value), and it is used like so:

```
const daysInAWeek = 7;
daysInAWeek;
```
Response: 7

You may be tempted to think that this `const` keyword is not necessary. Couldn't you accomplish the same task using `let` or `var`? Well, yes and no. You could write that same block of code using `let` or `var` and you'd get the same response, but there's something quite different when you use `const`. Type this in the console to see what I mean:

```
daysInAWeek = 8;
```
Response: `Uncaught TypeError: Assignment to constant variable.`

See? If you had created the `daysInAWeek` variable using either `var` or `let`, the interpreter would've had no problem letting you change it from 7 to 8. But because you used the `const` keyword, you've told the interpreter that this variable will keep the same value as a constant—it *cannot* be changed. Now if you type `daysInAWeek`; in the console, you'll get the same original result of 7.

So `const` should be used any time you do not want the value of the variable to be changed. As a developer, I personally find I use `const` about 3 or 4 times as often as I use `let`—and I never use `var` for anything anymore. Type these constant values to get the hang of using the `const` keyword:

```
const monthsPerYear = 12;
const myBirthday = '1981-06-30';
const milesAroundTheEquator = 24901;
const kilometersPerMile = 1.61;
const capitalOfPoland = 'Warsaw';
```

All of those examples are things that will *not* change (at least not through the course of running your code). So here's the rule of thumb when creating new variables: If you know that the value will not change, use `const`. If it might change, use `let`. And there's no good reason to use `var` for *any* of your code. `var` is a thing of the past; it's only in this book because you'll still see it in lots of code. Of the three, you should be using `const` the most.

Follow Along: Temperature Converter (Celsius to Fahrenheit)

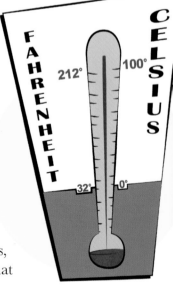

Time for another little project! As with all of the projects in this chapter, if you're able to do it yourself, you should try that first. If not, then feel free to type along with my solution. However, if you need to follow along with my answer—i.e., you wouldn't be able to do it entirely on your own—then at the end of it, I would like you to go back and see if you can do the whole thing again on your own from the beginning.

Here's the task: Your science project requires you to heat up liquids to different temperatures. The problem is that all of the temperatures are written in Celsius, and your thermometer only shows Fahrenheit. You need to create a function that will convert the given celsius temperature into a Fahrenheit temperature.

It might not surprise you to learn that Google did the hard work for us. Doing a quick Google search, we can determine that the formula for converting a Celsius temperature into Fahrenheit is this:

```
(celsiusTemp * 1.8) + 32;
```

So now we can just put that into a function like so:

```
function convertCelsiusToFahrenheit(celsiusTemp) {
    return (celsiusTemp * 1.8) + 32;
}
```

Let's test that out a couple times like this:

```
convertCelsiusToFahrenheit(45);
convertCelsiusToFahrenheit(0);
```

You could just call this done now. And you wouldn't necessarily be wrong to do so. But there's just a little problem. If you or someone else in the future were to look at this function, you might notice that the values seem...well...a little arbitrary. By that, I mean that 1.8 and 32 just look like some random numbers. Why those numbers? What do they mean? Could it work with 2.9 and 42 just as well? It seems like there should really be some explanations, don't ya think?

This is not uncommon. Sometimes, when there are confusing numbers like this, it's valuable for developers to write out explanations in a document—like an instruction manual. Where we find these code explanations typed out, we call this **documentation**.

This is a good time to introduce another good little rule-of-thumb. When you're dealing with numbers, it's almost always best to assign them to variable names. That way, when you or anyone else looks at your code, they'll be able to understand why you chose the numbers you did. It makes your code easier to read and understand, without the need for all the wordy documentation or many comments explaining what everything does. When code is written with useful variable names and function names, the code can basically explain its own purpose. We call this **self-documenting** code, and it's a good way to write.

So what do the 1.8 and 32 mean? Well, in this case, the 1.8 is what's known as the "conversion ratio" from Celsius to Fahrenheit. That just means it's "the number you need to multiply it by" when you're converting values to a different form. The 32 is the freezing point of water for Fahrenheit. The freezing point of water for Celsius is 0. For this lesson, it's not important why this works. Just note what the numbers represent, and note that these numbers do *not* change—they remain *constant*.

Once you know this, it's actually fairly easy to change the code to make it self-documenting. Simply press the **UP_ARROW** key a few times and update your function like so:

```
function convertCelsiusToFahrenheit(celsiusTemp) {
    const conversionRatio = 1.8;
    const fahrenheitFreezingPoint = 32;
    return (celsiusTemp * conversionRatio) + fahrenheitFreezingPoint;
}
```

Because we knew these numbers (1.8 and 32) would never change, we can call them constants—thus we initialized them with the **const** keyword and used explanatory variable names to make the code self-documenting (i.e., easy to read and understand what the values represent). Now let's try it out:

```
convertCelsiusToFahrenheit(100);    // 100
convertCelsiusToFahrenheit(15);     // 59
```

How did you do? Did you understand the thing about "self-documenting"? If not, just keep on reading. It's not a hugely important concept, but it is useful if you can figure it out.

DIY: Temperature Converter (Fahrenheit to Celsius)

Now that you've written a function to convert Celsius values to Fahrenheit, see if you can do the exact reverse! Write a function that will convert Fahrenheit values to Celsius. Hint: Your function will need to *first* subtract the `fahrenheitFreezingPoint` (which is the number `32`) and *then* divide by the `conversionRatio` (`1.8`).

If you do this properly, then you should be able to take the value from the first temperature converter and pass it in as an argument to the second temperature converter and get the original value back (or extremely close to it)!

Let me `confirm()`

Remember how I showed you the `alert()` function in chapter 4? And remember how I said that you should *not* include it in your code because your users would find it annoying? Seriously, what was the point of me teaching you something only to tell you not to use it?!

Hey, now that I think of it, there are *two more* built-in functions I'd like to teach you before telling you not to use them! The first one is called `confirm()` and you use it like this (type in the console):

```
confirm('Are you sure you wanna jump in a Minnesota lake on the 1st day of spring?');
```

Cool, huh? Now you might be asking yourself, "Why am I expected to learn something that I'll be told not to use?!" Well if so, you would be wrong. Now you might be thinking to yourself, "Huh? *Wrong?!* That doesn't make any sense!" And about that, you'd be right.

Here is another way that you might use this `confirm()` function:

```
if (confirm('Did your mom say "Yes"?')) {
    console.log("Great!  Grab your swimsuit and let's go!");
} else {
    console.log('Well, she prolly has your best in mind.');
}
```

So `confirm()` is a function that freezes everything in place in order to get confirmation from the user. The value returned by `confirm()` is always a boolean. If the user clicks the "OK" button, it's `true`; if he clicks the "Cancel" button, it's `false`. This is useful in code if, for example, the user clicks a delete button on a website. By using `confirm('Are you sure you want to delete this?')`, you can help the user avoid accidentally deleting something important. You'll see similar behavior on your own computer if you try to delete a file.

Follow Along: Did You Brush?

The local dentist Dr. Seymour N. Sizors has had just about enough of patients with bad breath. From now on, before any patient comes to see him, he'd like them to *confirm* that they brushed their teeth this morning. Can you create a simple function to help him out?

This'll be a quick one. If you think you might already know how to do this, try it on your own first. Otherwise, follow along with me:

```
function confirmTeethBrushed() {
    if (confirm('Did you brush your teeth this morning?')) {
        return 'Dr. Sizors will see you now.';
    } else {
        return 'Go brush your teeth first.  You can use the sink over there.';
    }
}
confirmTeethBrushed();
confirmTeethBrushed();
```

Simple as that!

DIY: Did You Also Floss?

Hmm...Now Dr. Sizors wants every patient to brush *and* floss before they come see him. What's next? Are the patients going to have to drill their own root canals? Sheesh...

So here's the gist of the requirements for this DIY: First, the patient must confirm whether or not she has brushed her teeth. If she hasn't, tell her to brush. If she has brushed her teeth, then confirm whether or not she has flossed. If she hasn't, tell her to floss. If she has, then she can see the dentist. If you get stuck, check the answer in the back of the book.

Listening for the prompt()

Alrighty now, there's *one more* built-in function I'd like to teach you before telling you not to use it (I'll explain why soon)! It's called **prompt()** and it goes like this:

```
prompt('What is your name?');
'Hello, ' + prompt('What is your name?') + '!';
'You are ' + prompt('How old are you?') + ' years old.';
```

So **prompt()** is a function that freezes everything in place and *prompts* the user to enter a value and then either click the "OK" button or the "Cancel" button. It's similar to **confirm()** except that **prompt()** returns a string (user input) whereas **confirm()** always returns a boolean. If the user clicks the "OK" button, the **prompt()** function will return a string containing the value he typed. If the user clicks the "Cancel" button, the **prompt()** function will return **null**.

Follow Along: Short-Order Cook

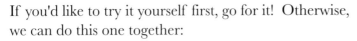

Open a new browser tab to start this project in the console on the `about:blank` page.

Your dad's best friend just started a new job as a short-order cook and he wants to practice his cooking skills with you! He can make anything you want! Create a function that will ask (a.k.a. "prompt") you, the user, to tell him your favorite meal and then log a message to the console affirming that he will make that for you!

If you'd like to try it yourself first, go for it! Otherwise, we can do this one together:

```javascript
function cookThis() {
    const faveMeal = prompt("What's your favorite meal?");
    console.log("Great! I'll start cooking your " + faveMeal + ' right now!');
}
cookThis();
cookThis();
cookThis();
```

By the third time you ran that `cookThis()` function, did you consider pressing the "Cancel" button? Or perhaps pressing "OK" without filling in the value? If you did, you might've noticed it said `"Great! I'll start cooking your null right now!"` That's not ideal.

We can improve on this one with a simple `if...else` block to account for the various inputs the user might try. Press the UP_ARROW a few times and change the function thusly:

```javascript
function cookThis() {
    const faveMeal = prompt("What's your favorite meal?");

    if (faveMeal) {
        console.log("Great! I'll start cooking your " + faveMeal + ' right now!');
    } else {
        console.log("Do you not have a favorite meal?  Okay, plate-of-dirt then!");
    }
}
cookThis();    // try using "Cancel" button
cookThis();    // try leaving the field empty
```

How'd you do? Did you follow all that logic? I hope so!

Okay so the question may still remain in your mind: "Why shouldn't we use `confirm()` and `prompt()`?" Well, the most correct answer is because they both block everything. No other code can continue to run until you get user input. I don't expect that to seem like a big deal to you at this early stage in your coding. Just know that it will be very meaningful to you farther in the future.

Admittedly, there is probably better reason to sometimes use `confirm()` than to use `prompt()`, and that's because `confirm()` can be a last line of defense before the user does something permanent (like if she clicks the button to delete her social media account). On the other hand, `prompt()` is just simply a bad user experience.

The other answer for why you shouldn't use `prompt()` in particular is because there are many better ways to make a comfortable experience for the user than to have a box pop up in his face and make him type in an answer before the box can go away.

However, the "better ways" to do this are a little more complicated than you're ready for just yet (I'll cover them in Volume 2 of the *Code for Teens* series). This is why I teach you to use `prompt()` and `confirm()` for now. Until we get to the more complicated ways, you can go ahead and continue to use `prompt()` to get user input. In fact, you should probably use it for the rest of the DIY projects in this section.

DIY: Exotic Soup Chef

Create a function that prompts the user three times asking for a different ingredient each time. Once the user has responded to all prompts (inputting three different ingredients), then return (or log to the console) the name of the special soup that is being prepared. The name should include all three ingredients such as "Carrot, Potato and Onion soup."

How `toFixed()` the Decimal Places

Here's another built-in function that helps with a simple little concept. If you ever need to round out a number to some exact number of decimal places, you'll find this function useful. It's called `toFixed()` and it's used like this (type along):

```
(8.111111).toFixed(); // invoked with no arguments (rounds to nearest integer)
(8.111111).toFixed(2); // invoked with a 2 passed-in
(8.8899).toFixed(); // invoked with no arguments (rounds to nearest integer)
(5.666667).toFixed(1);
let preciseNumber = 2 / 3; // 0.6666666666666666
preciseNumber.toFixed(3) // round to 3 digits = "0.667"
```

Notice that the return value after using `toFixed()` is always a string. See how it's surrounded by quotes? That's how you know.

This is a good way to deal with money. For instance, if you were trying to estimate the tax on a large purchase, you know that the final amount will never be less than a penny. So if taxes are 0.09 for every dollar, then the taxes for various items could be shown like this:

```
const taxRate = 0.09;
const decimalPoints = 2;
(2.35 * taxRate).toFixed(decimalPoints); // tax charged on a $2.35 item
(15.59 * taxRate).toFixed(decimalPoints);
(9.99 * taxRate).toFixed(decimalPoints);
```

Overall, `toFixed()` should be a relatively easy concept. You won't use it too much, but you'll often want it when doing any kind of math with money.

Follow Along: Tip Calculator (Constant Rate)

Open a new browser tab to start this project in the console on the `about:blank` page.

The manager at the local Thai restaurant, The Thai Tanic, is concerned that his customers aren't tipping their waitresses enough. He wants you to build a tip calculator to help them quit being so stingy. Here's how it should behave: When the function is invoked, the customer is *prompt*ed to input the total amount for her meal. When she does this, she should get a message stating the suggested tip amount (18% of the total meal cost).

In this project, the manager wants the rate to remain at 18% all the time. We can say this value is *constant* because it does not ever change. If it were to change based on different user input, we might call it variable or dynamic. Such as the case for the total price of the meal. That value is variable because it varies based on the user's input.

Note: Any percentage is actually a fraction of 100. This means that 18% is the same as 18/100. Another way of writing 18/100 is 0.18. So if you want 18% of some number, you can get it by multiplying that number by 0.18.

Now before going any further, ask yourself this question: "Could I possibly do this entirely on my own?" If so, then please read no further until you've given it your best shot. If you don't think you can do it entirely on your own, then I want you to do this: read the previous paragraph slowly and carefully. Do your best to understand everything that paragraph is trying to explain. Then, if you think you can at least do *some* of it on your own, then please do as much as you can before reading on.

Okay now, let's do this together! Hopefully, you've already tried this on your own, so we will see how close your version and mine turned out to be. We will start by creating a function that uses `prompt()` to get the total cost of the customer's meal.

```
function recommendedTip() {
    const tipPercentage = 18/100; // this could also be written as 0.18
    const totalMealCost = prompt('What is the total cost of your meal?');
    const decimalPlaces = 2; // money is usually rounded to 2 decimal places
    const tipAmount = (totalMealCost * tipPercentage).toFixed(decimalPlaces);

    return 'We recommend you tip $' + tipAmount;
}
recommendedTip();
recommendedTip();
recommendedTip();
```

So that's enough to solve the Follow Along project. Now see if you can improve on it with this DIY project...

DIY: Tip Calculator (Variable Rate)

For this DIY project, you may use the previous function as a starting place. Your task is to see if you can modify this function so that the 18% is not a hardcoded value. The improved tip calculator should prompt the user to give the tip percentage (in addition to the total meal cost) and then calculate the value based on that. Try it out now!

I hope you had fun with all these projects! The full-time job of a software engineer often involves similar kinds of projects—they're more complex, of course, and often more fun, but they're similar in the problem-solving approach. On top of that, engineers get to work as a team, so that makes it even more fun...and to top it all off, we get paid *really* well to do it! Now it's quiz time!

CHAPTER 7: QUIZ

The quiz this time is shorter since there weren't many new concepts. As always, write your answers down in your Workbook. When finished, check them against the back of the book.

1.   True/False: In JavaScript, an object is a collection of properties (named values).

2.   What method (function) can you use to convert a string to using all capital letters?

3.   What keyword should you use to create any variable that you know will not be changed?

4.   What glossary term refers to written-out explanations and examples for what code does and/ or how to use it?

5.   When should you use the `let` keyword in your own code?

6.   What built-in function(s) will cause the JavaScript interpreter to wait for the user to click a button before continuing with the rest of the code?

7.   What glossary term refers to code that has helpfully-named variables and descriptive function names so that it's easy for a developer to understand the purpose of the code as he reads it (without much need for explanatory comments)?

8.   What method can you use to convert a string to using all non-capital letters?

9.   When should you use the `var` keyword in your own code?

10.   True/False: when an object's property is a function, it goes by a special name: "mothered".

11.   What built-in function will cause the JavaScript interpreter to wait for the user to type information before continuing with the rest of the code?

12.   Which keyword will you probably use most of the time to create variables?

13. True/False: The `prompt()` function always returns a boolean.

14. True/False: Numbers in coding should usually be assigned to descriptive variable names to make their purpose easier to understand.

15. True/False: The `alert()`, `confirm()`, and `prompt()` functions are widely used by professionals because they create an elegant user experience.

CHAPTER 7: **KEY CONCEPTS**

Read this list and look back in the chapter to review anything you're not solid on:

- Object
- Property
- Method
- `toUpperCase()`
- `toLowerCase()`
- `const`
- Documentation
- Self-documenting code
- `confirm()`
- `prompt()`
- `toFixed()`

CHAPTER 7: **DRILLS**

A. Try typing these valid code snippets in the console

There isn't much mystery in the console responses this time. The more important point is that you should get used to typing these so that you'll remember them in the future.

1.
```
const litersPerGallon = 3.7854; // this ratio is constant (doesn't change)
litersPerGallon.toFixed(1);
```

2.
```
"uSerNAmeWiThWeirdCapITALizATioN".toLowerCase();
```

3.
```
let moneyValue = 1.5999; // this uses let keyword because it might change
if (confirm('Want to round this value to the nearest penny?')) {
    moneyValue = moneyValue.toFixed(2); // see?  changing.
}
console.log('Money value is $' + moneyValue);
```

```
4.    const averageMilesToTheMoon = 239000;

5.    const yourName = prompt("What's your name again?");
      console.log("It's great to see you again, " + yourName + '!');

6.    const anyVariableThatWillNotChange = 'should be initialized with const';

7.    (18.5).toFixed();

8.    'official patent office of the u.s.a.'.toUpperCase();

9.    let anyVariableThatMayChange = 'should be initialized with';
      anyVariableThatMayChange += ' the let keyword';
      anyVariableThatMayChange;

10.   const cleanAllTheThings = confirm('Clean ALL the things?');
      if (cleanAllTheThings) {
          console.log('All the things have been cleaned!');
      } else {
          console.log('Keep things as they are.');
      }

11.   /* pay attention to how this code is self-documenting;
      the variable names basically explain the code's purpose */
      const preTaxPrice = 17.99;
      const taxRate = 0.08;
      const costOfTaxAlone = preTaxPrice * taxRate;
      const fullPriceWithTax = preTaxPrice + costOfTaxAlone;
      const priceRounded = fullPriceWithTax.toFixed(2);
      if (confirm('Ready to pay this amount? ($' + priceRounded + ')')) {
          console.log('Thank you for your purchase!');
      } else {
          console.log("Okay, we'll cancel this order then.");
      }

12.   function isItSafeToShakeYourHand() {
          let safeToShake = false; // using let because it might change
          if (confirm('Are you someone I trust?')) {
              if (confirm('Are you feeling well today?')) {
                  safeToShake = true;
              } else {
                  const disease = prompt('What are you sick with?');
                  /* notice the NOT character (!) in the next line...
                     that makes it confirm the OPPOSITE (NOT contagious). */
                  if (!confirm('Is ' + disease + ' contagious?')) {
                      safeToShake = true;
                  } // no else is required because safeToShake is false already
              }
          }
          if (safeToShake) {
              return "Sure!  I'll shake your hand!";
          } else {
              return "I think I'll keep my distance.";
          }
      }

13.   isItSafeToShakeYourHand();
```

14. `isItSafeToShakeYourHand(); // choose different responses`

15. `isItSafeToShakeYourHand(); // choose different responses`

16. `isItSafeToShakeYourHand(); // choose different responses`

B. What's wrong with each of these code snippets?

1.
```
const timeOfDay = '1:30';
timeOfDay = '2:15'z;
```

2.
```
let abrahamLincolnDateOfBirth = '1809-02-12';
var georgeWashingtonDateOfBirth = '1732-02-22';
```

3.
```
const birthYear = confirm('What year were you born?');
```

4.
```
const allCapitalizedWords = 'all in caps'.toCapitalized();
```

5.
```
const exactDegreesForLaunchingMissileToSpace = 88.726484293724;
const extraPreciseAngle = exactDegreesForLaunchingMissileToSpace.toFixed();
```

6.
```
const x = 365; // remember, "x" is representing the days in a year;
const y = 7; // from now on, variable "y" is the number of days in a week;
const z = 24; // 24 is the hours in a day.  let's use "z" for that;
```

7.
```
if (prompt('Are you sure?')) {
    console.log('Okay!');
}
```

CHAPTER 7: AGGREGATE REVIEW

1. A value that isn't a boolean, but is treated as `false` for the purpose of conditional statements is said to be generally _____. If it were treated as `true` (though not a boolean), it is said to be generally _____.

2. What character can you *add* to this statement to avoid a Syntax Error?
```
const oldEricClaptonSong = 'I Can't Stand It';
```

3. What does DRY stand for in coding?

4. Is this a valid statement? (And if not, why not?)
```
const ninjaSkills = 'steps' !== 'can be heard';
```

5. What code might you use to get a string that represents a random number between `0` and `20` that is rounded to the nearest 2 decimal places?

6. Does this appear to accomplish the developer's intention? (And if not, why not?)
```
const secondsInAMinute = 60;
```

7. True/False: Block comments cause the JavaScript interpreter to ignore everything from the start of the comment to the end of the current line.

8. Which data type is this?
   ```
   'false'
   ```

9. What is the name for the primitive data type that means no value has been assigned?

10. What form of capitalization should you use with function names in JavaScript?

11. True/False: An effective way to handle a string containing apostrophes is to use double quotes on the outside (surrounding the string).

12. Is this a valid block of code? (And if not, why not?)
    ```
    const faveLetter = 'K';
    faveLetter = "R"; // changed my mind
    ```

13. What is a developer trying to arrive at when she uses modulo in an operation?

14. What's the value of `chosenActivity` after this line?
    ```
    const chosenActivity = 'homework' || 'eat snack' || 'play outside';
    ```

15. True/False: Error messages are intended to be human-readable so that developers can have clues to help in resolving the errors.

16. What does a single equals sign imply in a statement?

17. True/False: The `alert()`, `confirm()`, and `prompt()` functions are often avoided because they block all code from running until the user responds.

18. True/False: Users often find the behavior of the built-in functions `alert()`, `confirm()`, and `prompt()` to be annoying, so most professional web developers use alternative means to accomplish similar purposes.

19. What are the three keywords that may be used to declare a new variable?

20. What do you type in order to create a new line in the console (note: This also works in `alert()`, `confirm()`, and `prompt()` messages)?

21. Similar to the comparison operators, the _____ operators (`&&`, `||`, and `!`) work well in conditional statements.

22. Is this valid code (feel free to type it in the console)? (And if not, why not?)
    ```
    function isOldEnoughToStartKindergarten(childAge) {
        const minimumAge = 5;
        if (age > minimumAge) {
            console.log('Old enough!');
        } else {
            console.log('Too young!');
        }
    }
    isOldEnoughToStartKindergarten(5);
    ```

23. Is this valid JavaScript? (And if not, why not?)
```
function turnNumberIntoMoney(number) {
    return number.toFixed(2);
    console.log('Money version = $' + number.toFixed(2));
}
turnNumberIntoMoney(10 / 3);
```

24. What URL address should you go to in order to get an empty page in Chrome?

25. Chrome, Internet Explorer, Edge, Firefox, and Safari are all examples of _____.

26. True/False: `122 >= 122 && !(67 <= 68);`

27. What glossary term refers to code that has helpfully-named variables and descriptive function names so that it's easy for a developer to understand the purpose of the code as he reads it (without the need for explanatory comments)?

28. What is the symbol for the logical operator that always returns a boolean (when placed before a falsy value, it returns true; before a truthy value, it returns false)?

29. The values `null`, `false`, `''`, `0`, and `undefined` are all _____; whereas `true`, `'string'`, and `1` are all _____ values.

30. True/False: Comparison operators always result in a boolean value.

DIY: Letter Grade Generator

Create a function that prompts the user for a number grade and returns a letter grade. The user should input a number value between 0 and 100. If the value is greater than or equal to 90, return the message stating that the user earned a grade of "A". Otherwise (else), if the value is greater than or equal to 80, the user gets a "B". If it's 70 or above, "C". If it's 60 or higher, "D". Anything else should result in an "F" grade. You should be able to do this on your own, but if you need help, my answer is in the back of the book for your reference. Enjoy!

8 | HIP HIP ARRAY!

Wasn't it fun doing all those projects in the last chapter? Projects are a great way to test out what you know and improve on some of the practical skills.

In this chapter, we'll learn about one of the most fundamental skills in all programming languages—the skill of working with lists of things. Let's get started!

Oh! I almost forgot! Before we start, close down all programs. Then open the browser console on a blank page again (as always, if you forget a step in here, refer to chapter 1).

Done? Okay, NOW let's get started!

Arrays: The Basics

What is an Array?

Okay now, lean in close 'cuz this is a big one! An **array** in JavaScript (and other programming languages) is basically a list of values in a specific order. An array is used to store multiple values in a single variable.

An array looks like this (type along in the console):
```
const zooAnimals = ['lion', 'tiger', 'bear'];
```

The name of the variable is usually plural because it's a collection of items. Now that you have created an array, you can view it in the console by typing its name:

```
zooAnimals;
```
Response: (3) ["lion", "tiger", "bear"]

Let's analyze this response from the console for a bit. It begins with a `3` inside of parens: `(3)`. Can you guess what that is?...You can? Great! What's your guess?...The number of wheels on a tricycle?! Umm...While that is *technically* true, that's really not the answer I was looking for, sorry. In this example, the `(3)` represents the *length*—the number of items in the array. That's a little more practical for our purposes, isn't it?

```
 ⊘   top                    ▼    Filter

> const zooAnimals = ['lion', 'tiger', 'bear'];
<  undefined
> zooAnimals;
<  ▶ (3) ["lion", "tiger", "bear"]
> |
```

Now look closely at the console. Do you notice a little triangle to the left of the `(3)`? That triangle is pointing to the right like a "play" button on a DVD player...a DVD player? Oh...that's an old-time device that would play physical discs that usually only contained one movie on them and some special features. Ask your parents about it sometime.

```
> const zooAnimals = ['lion', 'tiger', 'bear'];
<  undefined
> zooAnimals;          triangle points down
<  ▼ (3) ["lion", "tiger", "bear"] ℹ
     0: "lion"          index positions
     1: "tiger"
     2: "bear"
     length: 3  ← Number of items
     ▶ __proto__: Array(0)
>              Bears are dangerous
```

Go ahead and click on that triangle. It now points down, and the array is shown vertically. Now each item in the array has a number to the left of it. That number represents that specific item's index. The **index** of an array is the number representing any given item's position in that array. And get this: it starts with the number 0 (not the number 1)! So the item at position 0 is what you would call the *first* item in the array. You'll also see the `length` of the array as a *property* in there. Remember this, and we'll come back to it.

In the case of this `zooAnimals` array, the items are all strings, but they wouldn't have to be. The items in an array might be any data type or even a mix of data types. Here are some other valid arrays:

```
const booleanValues = [true, false];
const primeNumbers = [2, 3, 5, 7, 11, 13];
const allTheFalsyValues = [ // mixed array (notice this one is on multiple lines)
    false, // boolean data type
    0, // number data type
```

```
    null, // null data type
    "", // string data type
    undefined // undefined data type
];
const inceptionArray = [ // array with arrays inside of it!!  Crazy, huh?
    ['first', 'inner', 'array'],
    ['second', 'inner', 'array'],
    ['inner', 'array', ['even', 'deeper']]
];
```

How Do You Access Items in an Array?

Once you have an array you like, you can access each of its
items individually by using brackets with the specific item's index
(remember from the screenshot above?). This index position
goes inside of square brackets [] when retrieving the item.
Try this:

```
zooAnimals[0]; // lion
zooAnimals[1]; // tiger
zooAnimals[2]; // bear
```

What's the third prime number? (Remember that the "third"
number would be at index 2 since indexing always starts with 0.)

```
primeNumbers[2]; // 3rd number in the array is at index 2
primeNumbers[5]; // 6th number in the sequence is at index
5
```

You can even put a variable inside of the square brackets as long as the variable resolves to an
integer (a whole number without a fraction) that is equal to or greater than zero.

```
let itemIndex = 2; // using 'let' keyword because we intend to change it
zooAnimals[itemIndex]; // bear
itemIndex = 0;
zooAnimals[itemIndex]; // lion
```

So this is what's known as "accessing members of an array." Do you understand how to do that? If
not, read it one more time before continuing on. It's important.

How Do You Change Items in an Array?

If you were paying close attention to the arrays we created before, you may have noticed that the
zooAnimals array was created using the const keyword. So this means that it's constant, right? And
if it's constant, that means it can't be changed, right? Of course it does. What else could it mean?

Hey...wanna see a trick? Type this in the console:

```
zooAnimals[0] = 'kitten';
zooAnimals;
```

Whoa! How did that happen?! The `zooAnimals` array has been changed?! I thought `zooAnimals` was a constant! We used the `const` keyword and everything! What's going on here? It's like the whole world has gone topsy-turvy! Up is down; left is right; what are we to think—?

Snap out of it! There's no need to overreact. Here's what happened: the `zooAnimals` constant points to a specific array. You can't reassign the variable to anything else. Try this, and you'll still get the error you've come to expect:

```
zooAnimals = ['some', 'different', 'array'];
```
Response: `Uncaught TypeError: Assignment to constant variable.`

The constant `zooAnimals` is still constantly pointing to one array. All you've done is changed one of the *members* of the array. As long as you're not trying to assign a different value to the `zooAnimals` variable, you're fine. In fact, you can go even further. Keep reading...

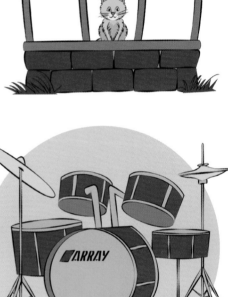

How Do You Count the Number of Items in an Array?

Let's create a new array and do some fancy things with it!

```
const rockBandInstruments = [
    'guitar',
    'drums',
    'bass'
];
```

So we know that there are three items in this array, right? We can count them easily. Well, what if we could not count them easily? Like what if there were hundreds of items? How would we know exactly how long the list is? That's where we bring in a cool little built-in property of arrays called `length` (remember this from the screenshot above?).

```
rockBandInstruments.length // 3
```

As you'll hopefully recall from the last chapter, when you see that little dot (the period) between the object (in this case, the array) and the word following it, that tells you that the next word represents a property (a named value that is attached to an object). You may also remember the `length` property (sometimes written as `.length`) from the last chapter when we used it to see how many characters were in a string. Well now that we're working with arrays, the `length` property instead shows us how many items are in the array.

Also, just like with strings, arrays have some built-in properties that are functions to be called with parens. Whenever a property is a function, there's a special name for it. Remember what that name is? No? Okay,

I'll remind you this time, but after this, I expect you to remember it on your own because it's important! A function that is attached to an object (a string, an array, etc.) is called a *method*.

Now, back to subject at hand: we know that `rockBandInstruments` has a `.length` property of 3—this means there are 3 items in the array.

How Do You Add Items to an Array?

We have already seen that we can change one of the items like so:

```
rockBandInstruments[2] = 'bass guitar';
```

Now here's another cool trick: we can add items to the list like this:

```
rockBandInstruments[3] = 'keyboard';
rockBandInstruments.length;
rockBandInstruments;
```

We just added a 4th item to the array by simply assigning a new string to position 3!

Here's another good way to add an item to an array: we'll use a *method* called `.push()`--remember, we know it's a *method* (function) because it has parens.

```
rockBandInstruments.push('microphone');
rockBandInstruments;
```

This `.push()` method is nice because it doesn't require you to know what index position the new item is going in at. It just adds the new item to the end of the array.

How Do You Remove Items from an Array?

Just like you can add items to the end of an array with the `.push()` method, you can also remove items from the end of the array with the `.pop()` method. Using `.pop()` will remove the last item from the array (thus reducing the length of the array by one item):

```
rockBandInstruments.length; // 5 items
rockBandInstruments.pop(); // this will return the last item ("microphone")
rockBandInstruments.length; // 4 items in the array
```

Another thing to know about `.pop()` is that it also has a *return* value. This means that when you use `.pop()`, the method will not only modify the array (removing the last item), but it will also *return* the last item in the array. When a function has a return value, you can then assign that value to a variable like this:

```
rockBandInstruments.length; // 4 instruments in the array
const angelWillPlay = rockBandInstruments.pop(); // assign "keyboard"
const nehaWillPlay = rockBandInstruments.pop(); // assign "bass guitar"
const tonyWillPlay = rockBandInstruments.pop(); // assign "drums" to tonyWillPlay
```

```
const iWillPlay = rockBandInstruments.pop(); // assign "guitar"
rockBandInstruments.length; // 0 instruments left in the array
console.log("Our band has four members:  Angel (" + angelWillPlay + "), "
    + "Neha (" + nehaWillPlay + "), "
    + "Tony (" + tonyWillPlay + "), "
    + " and me (" + iWillPlay + ").  Are you ready to rock?!");
```

Arrays: Some Fancy Stuff

Is There Anything Else I Can Do With an Array?

Are you kidding? There's *tons* of stuff you can do with an array! I don't want to get bogged down in too many details, but here are a few.

You saw how you could use `.pop()` to take an item from the *end* of the array. You can also use `.shift()` to take an item from the *beginning* of the array.

```
// we're using the keyword "let" because we're actually going to change it later
let laundryHamper = ['pants', 'shirt', 'underwear', 'socks'];
const wearAgain = laundryHamper.shift(); // still clean
console.log('What are these ' + wearAgain + " doing in the hamper?  They're clean!");
laundryHamper; // notice that the first item is no longer in the list
```

Remember how you used `.push()` to add an item to the *end* of the array? Well, you can use `.unshift()` to add an item to the *beginning* of the array.

```
laundryHamper.unshift('towel');
laundryHamper;
```

So remember these rules of thumb when working with arrays:

`.push(newArrayItem)` is used to *add* a new item to the *end* of the array.
`.pop()` is used to *remove*—and return—the item at the *end* of the array.
`.unshift(newArrayItem)` is used to *add* a new item to the *beginning* of the array.
`.shift()` is used to *remove*—and return—the item at the *beginning* of the array.

You can use `.toString()` to quickly turn the array into a string with each of the values separated by commas:

```
console.log('Here are all the items in the hamper: ' + laundryHamper.toString());
```

If you want to make a string out of all of the items in the array, but you don't want commas as the **separator** (the string that goes in between each item), you can use `.join()` and pass in a string argument to tell the interpreter what you would like to be the separator instead.

```
console.log('My laundry hamper contains a ' + laundryHamper.join(' and ') + '.');
```

Once you've converted an array into a string, you can use any of the available string methods. We discussed a handful of these methods in the last chapter, such as `.repeat()`, `.toUpperCase()`, `.toLowerCase()`, etc.

As a side note, I want to be clear about something. When I use phrases such as "convert an array to a string," you should know that the `.join()` method isn't actually converting anything. The `laundryHamper` variable still holds an array. The `.join()` method actually creates and *returns a new* string. But we can then assign that string to a variable or otherwise use it for any purpose we need. This might sound like splitting hairs, but it will sometimes be an important distinction to understand when you're writing your own code.

Nice! What else?

You can also combine two arrays together using the built-in `.concat()` method like so:

```
const yesterdaysLaundry = ['sweatshirt', 'underwear', 'striped socks', 'headband'];
laundryHamper.concat(yesterdaysLaundry); // notice the long array that was returned!
laundryHamper; // Huh?!  It's the same clothes as before?!
```

Gotcha! The `laundryHamper` array was not actually *changed* by the `.concat()` method! The `.concat()` method *returned* a new array with both arrays combined, but we didn't do anything with it, so both arrays remained the same. Remember how we initialized the `laundryHamper` variable with the `let` keyword instead of `const`? This is why. We're actually going to overwrite it with the longer array that is returned from the `.concat()` method.

```
laundryHamper = laundryHamper.concat(yesterdaysLaundry); // reassign it!
laundryHamper; // look at how many more clothes we have in the hamper now!
```

Did that make sense? You might want to read it again as that's kind of a tricky part.

By the way, since your mom is super picky about your laundry hamper being sorted in alphabetical order (That's a thing, right?), we have a `.sort()` method for arrays! Unlike the `.concat()` method, this one actually modifies the original array (in addition to returning it).

```
laundryHamper.sort();
console.log("Here's my sorted laundry: " + laundryHamper.join(', '));
```

Also, keep in mind that a sorted array still functions just like any other array, so you can still return items from it by using their index positions:

```
laundryHamper.sort()[0]; // return the 1st item in the sorted array
laundryHamper.sort()[3]; // return the 4th item in the sorted array
```

Is That All?

And that's not all! You can get a new array from any string by calling the `.split()` method on it and passing in the string that you want to separate on. For example, if your string has asterisks between each word (`'my*starry*string'`) and you want an array with three items in it (`['my',`

137

'starry', 'string']), you can simply use `.split('*')` passing in the asterisk. Then the JavaScript interpreter will return a new array based on the string and will look for each asterisk in the string to know where one array item ends and the next begins.

Try out these examples in the console and notice the arrays that are returned for each:

```
'my*starry*string'.split('*');
'string,wishes,it were,an array'.split(','); // every comma starts a new array item
'make each word into an array item'.split(' '); // pass in a single space
'Leonardo|Donatello|Rafael|Michaelangelo'.split('|');
```

And here is arguably the most useful application of the `.split()` method. Call `.split('')` (passing in an empty string) to divide your string into an array of individual characters!

```
'ABCDEFGHIJKLM'.split(''); // pass in an empty string for an array of characters!
```

While we're on the subject of usefulness, I must tell you about another very useful trick called **chaining** methods (functions). Chaining is repeatedly calling one method after another on an object, in one continuous line of code. Try it out:

```
/* convert this string 'bfdagec' to UPPERCASE // 'BFDAGEC'
*   split it into an array of characters // ['B', 'F', 'D', 'A', 'G', 'E', 'C']
*   sort the array in alphabetical order // ['A', 'B', 'C', 'D', 'E', 'F', 'G']
*   join back together with a dash between each character // 'A-B-C-D-E-F-G'
*   all in a single line of code! Awesome!!
*/
'bfdagec'.toUpperCase().split('').sort().join('-'); // 'A-B-C-D-E-F-G';
```

 Isn't that cool? Now at this point, it would be wise to ask yourself: "Why does this work?" This is a good question that will serve you well in your future. Understanding *why* concepts like chaining work will help you to discover lots of new concepts on your own. But it starts with fully understanding what each of the methods do individually.

For example, even if I had never taught you about chaining, there is a way you might have figured it out on your own. I'd like to walk you through that thought process. Please read this next part carefully.

Suppose your teacher asks for help sorting and displaying your classmates' letter grades on a recent quiz. She wants to display a breakdown of how the class did overall. She currently has a string of text representing each of the grades like this: `"c,a,f,b,c,d,f,c,b,a,f,d,f,c,d,a,f,d"`. But she wants a string sorted and formatted like `"A | A | A | B | B | C ... (etc.)"`.

That sounds like kind of a tedious job, right? But oh well, you could probably do it manually with a piece of paper in a few minutes. Just be sure that you're very careful when you count the letters and everything. Oh but wait...This isn't a one-time job. Your teacher just said she needs this done every week following your class's Friday afternoon quiz. And five other teachers want the *exact same* work done for their classes. And it's crucial that you make no mistakes! Gosh, this tedious job just got downright exhausting!

Thankfully, if you understand what I've taught so far, you should be able to create one single line of chained JavaScript methods to do the job! So let's walk through this. At first, you want to convert all the lowercase letters to uppercase, right? That's easy:

```
const letterGrades = 'c,a,f,b,c,d,f,c,b,a,f,d,f,c,d,a,f,d';
letterGrades.toUpperCase(); // returns "C,A,F,B,C,D,F,C,B,A,F,D,F,C,D,A,F,D"
```

Now think about this for a moment: What did that `.toUpperCase()` method actually do? You might be tempted to say, "It converted the `letterGrades` to uppercase...d'uh." Well, you would be wrong. The `letterGrades` string is a `const`—it *can't* be changed! Instead of changing `letterGrades`, the `.toUpperCase()` method actually *returned* a *new* string.

Now why is that significant? Because once we have a new string, we can run any string methods we can think of on that new string. So both of these two methods should produce the same result:

```
'C,A,F,B,C,D,F,C,B,A,F,D,F,C,D,A,F,D'.split(','); // returns the same thing as...
letterGrades.toUpperCase().split(',');
```
Response: `["C", "A", "F", "B", "C", "D", "F", "C", "B", "A", "F", "D", "F", "C", "D", "A", "F", "D"]`

Now ask yourself this question: "If the `.toUpperCase()` method *always returns a new string*, what does the `.split()` method always do?"

If you said, "It always returns a new *array*!" then go to the head of the class! (...and stand at your teacher's desk awkwardly until she sends you back to your assigned seat.) You're correct! The `.split()` method always returns a new array. And once you have a new array, you can use any array methods or properties you can think of on that array. For instance:

```
letterGrades.toUpperCase().split(',').length; // returns number of items in the array
letterGrades.toUpperCase().split(',')[0]; // returns the first item
letterGrades.toUpperCase().split(',')[9]; // returns the tenth item
letterGrades.toUpperCase().split(',').toString(); // convert to string
letterGrades.toUpperCase().split(',').push('K'); // add new item
letterGrades.toUpperCase().split(',').pop(); // remove and return the last item
```

So there are many things we can do with an array, right? But what specifically did our teacher say she wants next? She wants them sorted! Remember how to sort an array?

```
letterGrades.toUpperCase().split(',').sort(); // sort alphabetically
```

Because `.sort()` returns an array, we have another new array that is sorted alphabetically. All we have left to do is turn it back into a string with " | " (a space followed by a pipe followed by another space) in between each element. Remember how to do that?

```
letterGrades.toUpperCase().split(',').sort().join(' | ');
```
Response: `"A | A | A | B | B | C | C | C | C | D | D | D | D | F | F | F | F | F"`

And just like that, we have the solution to your teacher's problem! We can even put this in a function so the other teachers can use it whenever they need to format letter grades!

```
function formatGrades(mixedUpLetterGrades) {
    return mixedUpLetterGrades.toUpperCase().split(',').sort().join(' | ');
}
```

```
formatGrades('d,b,b,a,a,c,f,d,b,f,a,b,b,c,a,d'); // Ms. Balanseen's class
formatGrades('a,b,a,a,c,a,a,a,b,a,b,a,a,b,b,a,a'); // Mrs. Eeziay's class
formatGrades('c,d,f,b,f,d,f,c,f,d,d,f,f,c,d,b,f'); // Dr. Wade Tootuff's class
```

With chaining, you can do lots of useful things with arrays and strings. In this short example, we used a string as the basis for returning a new modified (uppercase) string; then we used that string to create an array; then used that array to create a new (sorted) array; then used that new array to create another string! All in a single line! Try out some of these other cool chaining tricks in the console:

```
'How many words are in this sentence?'.split(' ').length
'1-2-3-'.repeat(6).split('-').sort().toString();
const sentences = 'Here are two sentences. How many words are in each?';
sentences.split('. ')[0].split(' ').length; // words in 1st sentence
sentences.split('. ')[1].split(' ').length; // words in 2nd sentence
'She loves me... not :-('.split('...')[0].concat(' a lot!').toUpperCase();
```

Pretty nifty huh? But read on...There's even *more* that you can do with arrays!!

Okay, That's Enough! Array Overload!

Oh...hmm...I guess we have covered a lot so far, haven't we? Believe it or not, there are *many* more useful things you can do with arrays. This chapter is just scratching the surface. To be honest, I actually haven't even mentioned the very best use for arrays yet...but I suppose I can save that for the next chapter.

My 11-year-old son helped me test out this book, and he pointed out that we've covered a *lot* of ground in the last few pages. This would probably be a good time to go back and just skim over each of the various array methods just to be sure you recognize them when you see them. Do you know what each of these methods does: `.push()`, `.pop()`, `.shift()`, `.unshift()`, `.toString()`, `.join()`, `.concat()`, `.sort()`, and `.split()`?

If you feel pretty good about these methods, then let's try a project using some of the things we've learned! Before moving on, open the console in a new `about:blank` tab in Chrome.

Follow Along: Track Team Tryouts

It's time for track team tryouts! And guess who's been chosen to keep track of the results for the qualifying race? You! Your school has asked you to keep a running list (no pun intended) of the racers in the order that they finish the qualifying race. You'll need to add a name to the list each time a racer crosses the finish line.

Well, I don't know about you, but anytime I hear the word "list," I think of an array. So let's start by making an empty array for results (note: We'll do this project without creating a custom function).

```
let raceResults = []; // using 'let' keyword because we'll be reassigning it
```

Hey look! Our first racer, Alan, just crossed the finish line! Let's add him to the results!

```
raceResults[0] = 'Alan';
```

Alright! Four more racers—Bernardo, Cecil, Derrek, and Emilio—have finished! Let's add all four of them in a single line. (Good thing we used the `let` keyword earlier!)

```
raceResults = raceResults.concat(['Bernardo', 'Cecil', 'Derrek', 'Emilio']);
```

And here come the last two racers—Friedrick and Gordon—huffing and puffing across the finish line. Let's add them one at a time to the end of our list:

```
raceResults.push('Friedrick');
raceResults.push('Gordon');
```

Hold it! The coach says that our team can only consist of the top 5 racers to finish. How many do we have so far?

```
console.log('We currently have ' + raceResults.length + ' racers on the list.');
```

Seven? Oh gosh...This is going to break Friedrick's heart. He trained for this all month. Well, we have to do what we have to do. Let's remove our racers from the end of the list.

```
raceResults.pop(); // there goes Gordon (he didn't care anyway... he hates running)
// now it's time for the hard one... poor Friedrick...
```

Wait! This just in! Turns out Alan was taking performance-enhancing drugs! Jeez, Alan, why can't you play by the rules? Alan is disqualified! Remove him from the *front* of the list!

```
const disqualifiedCheater = raceResults.shift();
```

Now, how many racers do we have?

```
console.log('We currently have ' + raceResults.length + ' racers on the list.');
```

We're down to five! So Friedrick made the cut! Hooray! We ready to post the list?

Oops! Not yet...We have a spelling error. Turns out one of our racers is named "Derrick" (not "Derrek"). Hmm...How can we correct the spelling of his name? Well, first we need to determine what index position he is at. Now that Alan is gone, the name "Derrek" is the third item in the array. Since the index positions start with 0, this puts the third item at position 2. Let's use that to update his name:

```
raceResults[2] = 'Derrick';
```

Okay, now we're ready to post the list!

```
console.log("Our new track team: " + raceResults.join(', ') + ". Congratulations!");
```

So how was it? Were you able to follow along well with that project? There are some concepts that are crucial to understand when learning any programming language. Arrays is one of those concepts. If you don't feel like you understand all this yet, please go back and try this chapter again from the beginning before moving on (it won't take you nearly as long the second time because you've already done most of the time-consuming stuff). Also go ahead and play around in the console. Create your own arrays and manipulate them using the methods we've explored so far. When you feel you're ready, then move on to the quiz section.

Do the whole quiz in your Workbook without looking back at the chapter. After you're finished, ask a parent to check your answers against the back of the book (or check them yourself if no parent is available). Then go back and fix any that you missed.

1.   What is the JavaScript name for a list of values in a specific order?

2.   What does the `.length` of an array refer to?

3.   The _____ in an array is the number representing any given item's position in the array.

4.   To retrieve the first item in an array, what value should go between the square brackets?
     `myArray[    ];`

5.   True/False: An array may contain a mix of different data types.

6.   What built-in method can you use to add a new item to the end of an array?

7.   True/False: When using `myArray.toString()` on an array, the return value will be a <u>string</u> that includes all of the items from the array separated by <u>semicolons</u>.

8.   Using the `.pop()` method on an array will _____ and _____ the last item of the array.

9.   True/False: After running this code, the `textbooks` array will have a `.length` of 4.

     ```
     const textbooks = ['english', 'biology'];
     textbooks.concat(['math', 'spanish']);
     ```

10. What glossary term refers to the practice of repeatedly calling one method after another on an object, in one continuous line of code?

11. Answer this before testing it out in the console: What will be the result of this code?
     ```
     const sewingSupplies = ['thread', 'needle', 'thimble'];
     sewingSupplies.sort()[1];
     ```

12. True/False: When using `myArray.join("\n")` on an array, the string `"\n"` is known as the <u>separator</u>: the string that will go between each array item.

13. The `.unshift()` method can be used to add an item to the beginning of the array while the _____ method will take an item off the beginning of the array.

14. What value will be returned from the following line?

```
const hairProducts = ['shampoo', 'hairspray', 'gel'];
const myFaveProductIndex = 2;
hairProducts[myFaveProductIndex];
```

15.   True/False: When using `myArray.join(' or ')` on an array, the return value will be a new *array* that includes all of the items from the original array separated by the string `" or "`.

16.   Answer this before testing it out in the console: what will be the result of this code?
```
['D', 'C', 'A', 'B'].toString().toLowerCase().split(',').sort()[3];
```

17.   True/False: On a technical level, the `.join()` method does not actually convert an array to a string, but rather creates a new string based on the values from the array.

18.   Answer this before testing it out in the console: What will be the result of this code?
```
const beatboxingLyrics = 'boots & cats & boots & cats & boots & cats';
beatboxingLyrics.split(' & ').sort()[2].length;
```

CHAPTER 8: **KEY CONCEPTS**

Read this list and look back in the chapter to review anything you're not solid on:

- Array
- `.length`
- Index
- `.push()`
- `.pop()`
- `.shift()`
- `.unshift()`
- `.toString()`
- `.join()`
- Separator
- `.concat()`
- `.sort()`
- `.split()`
- Chaining

CHAPTER 8: DRILLS

A. Try typing these valid code snippets in the console

Type these in the console and pay attention to the syntax (look up this word in the glossary if you've forgotten what it means). Try to guess what the response will be for each.

1.
```
const morningRoutine = [
    'wake up',
    'shower',
    'get dressed',
    'brush teeth'
];
```

2.
```
morningRoutine.shift();  // this one is obvious; no need to schedule it.
```

3.
```
morningRoutine.sort();   // hmm... why are my clothes soaking wet?...
alert("Here's my routine so far: " + morningRoutine.join(' then ') + '.');
```

4.
```
morningRoutine.push('make my own lunch');
```

5.
```
morningRoutine[0] = 'shower'; // let's swap the order of these two
morningRoutine[2] = 'brush teeth';
```

6.
```
morningRoutine.pop(); // mom says she can do this one for me!  Thanks, mom!
```

7.
```
morningRoutine.unshift('eat breakfast'); // before brushing teeth
```

8.
```
'I have ' + morningRoutine.length + ' things to do in the morning.';
```

9.
```
const indexOfThingIKeepForgetting = 3;
"Don't forget to " + morningRoutine[indexOfThingIKeepForgetting] + '!';
```

10.
```
const stuffIForgot = ['get books', 'make bed', 'fix hair'];
```

11.
```
console.log('My old morning routine included "' + morningRoutine.toString()
    + '" but now it\'s "'
    + morningRoutine.concat(stuffIForgot).join(', ') + '".');
```

12.
```
'Head, Shoulders, Knees, and Toes'.split(', ').sort().join(', ');
```

13.
```
const songLyric = 'There was a farmer had a dog, and Bingo was his name-o';
songLyric.split(' ')[8].toUpperCase().split('').join('-');
```

14.
```
'Rockabye, Baby '.split(', ')[1].concat('Grandpa Shark'.split(' ')[1]);
```

B. What's wrong with each of these code snippets?

1.
```
const nuts = ['cashew', 'almond', 'peanut'];
console.log('The list includes ' + nuts.size + ' different kinds of nuts!');
```

2.
```
//retrieve the third item in the nuts array
'The third kind of nut is ' + nuts[3];
```

3.
```
nuts.pull('hazelnut'); // add to the end
```

4.
```
console.log('array has ' + nuts.pop().length + ' items in it.');
```

5.
```
nuts.unpop('brazil nut'); // add to beginning
```

6.
```
let fullList = nuts.toString();
fullList.shift(); // remove the first nut in the list
```

7.
```
const moreNuts = ['walnut', 'pecan', 'pine nut'];
nuts.concat(moreNuts);
console.log('We have added more nuts to the list!: ' + nuts.join(', '));
```

8.
```
let alphabeticalNuts = nuts.order();
```

9.
```
nuts = nuts.concat(moreNuts).sort().toString();
```

CHAPTER 8: AGGREGATE REVIEW

1. Is this a valid statement? (And if not, why not?)
```
const haveYourCake = !!'And eat it too';
```

2. What are the data types (in order) for each of these falsy values?
```
0; null; undefined; ''; false;
```

3. A JavaScript string is made up of individual _____.

4. What function can you use to convert a string to using all capital letters?

5. There are three different _____ operators (`&&`, `||`, and `!`).

6. The _____ operators we use are `===`, `!==`, `>`, `>=`, `<`, and `<=`.

7. What keyword should you use to create any variable that you know will not be changed?

8. What general kind of statement in coding is used to perform certain blocks of code based on a given *condition*?

9. If you call a function inside of another function, the inner function is said to be _____ within the outer function.

10. Is this valid code (feel free to type it in the console)? (And if not, why not?)
```
function shouldIWearALightJacket(temperature) {
    const minTemp = 45; // degrees fahrenheit
    const maxTemp = 67;
    if (temperature >= minTemp && temperature <= maxTemp) {
        return 'Perfect weather for a light jacket!';
```

```
        }
        if (temperature > maxTemp) {
            return 'Too hot for a jacket.';
        }
        return 'Too cold for a light jacket.  Wear a heavy coat!';
}
shouldIWearACoat(70);
shouldIWearACoat(55);
shouldIWearACoat(40);
shouldIWearACoat(67);
```

11.   True/False: logical operators always result in a boolean value.

12.   What built-in function(s) will cause the JavaScript interpreter to wait for the user to click a button before continuing with the rest of the code?

13.   What special symbol could you use to simplify this assignment?
```
currentRound = currentRound + 1;
```

14.   Which mathematical operator would be most useful for checking if a given value is evenly divisible by 14?

15.   When should you use the `var` keyword in your own code?

16.   Which of these values are truthy? And what are the data types (in order) for each of the values?
```
-1; '  '; true; 5; '0'; 'false';
```

17.   Is this valid code? (And if not, why not?)
```
function nameGame(name) {
    return "Let's play the name game with " + name + '!';
    return name + ', ' + name + ', Bo ' + name + '...';
}
nameGame('Benjamin McGillicutty III');
```

18.   Which comparison operator returns `false` if the value on the left is greater than or equal to the value on the right?

19.   Where can a developer type simple JavaScript commands to test them out and get immediate responses?

20.   What part of your face is used for seeing things?

21.   True/False: Numbers in coding should usually be assigned to descriptive variable names to make their purpose easier to understand. For example, instead of `rideBus(5)`, better to write `const schoolDays = 5; rideBus(schoolDays);`.

22.   _____ refers to the process of repeatedly calling one method after another on an object, in one continuous line of code.

23.   What key should you press to indent your code inside a function?

24.   What built-in property can you use to find out how many items are in an array?

25. True/False: When there are multiple parens nested inside of one another, you should always evaluate the statements *from the inside out* (i.e. process the results of the values for the inner parens before processing those for the outer parens).

26. True/False: Comparison operators always result in a boolean value.

27. Is this valid JavaScript? (And if not, why not?)
```
function gimmeFive(number) {
    return 5;
}
gimmeFive(8);
```

28. What built-in function can you use to round a float (number with a decimal point) down to the nearest integer (number without a decimal point)?

29. What built-in method can you use to add a new item to the end of an array?

30. True/False: `215 >= -622 && !(812 <= 812) || !!(-389 < 389);`

31. True/False: The JavaScript interpreter ignores Code that is in comments.

32. What's the value of `anyGuy` after this line?
```
const anyGuy = 'Tom' || 'Dick' || 'Harry';
```

33. What key combination can you press to get a break return (new line) in the console?

34. What can you type to retrieve the name "Naomi"?
```
const popularRichGirls = ['Jennifer', 'Vanessa', 'Naomi', 'Priscilla'];
```

35. True/False: The `confirm()` function always returns a boolean.

DIY: Trick-or-Treat!

For this DIY project, you'll create several individual lines of code; each one will use at least one of the array concepts discussed in this chapter. If you struggle with any aspect, refer back to the Follow Along project for help as this project is very similar to that one. For bonus points, try wrapping all the logic in a function declaration; then call it at the end!

It's Halloween! You are so excited to show off your costume this year and go trick-or-treating with your friends! Last year, some of your candy mysteriously disappeared, so you intend to keep a close eye on it this year! Here's what happens with your *list* of candy (write JavaScript code representing each event).

- Before leaving your house, you put a Kit-Kat and Twizzlers in your Halloween bucket.
- At the first house you get a Snickers bar.
- At the next house, you get a Butterfinger, then an Almond Joy.
- At the next house, you get M&M's! Your favorite! You put this at the *top* of your candy stash so it's easy to see and remind you how lucky you are!

- You decide to eat the Almond Joy (the last candy bar on the list).
- Your friend Fletcher asks if he could trade you his full size Starburst packet for your Twizzlers. You happily make that trade, since you got the way better end of that deal! (Note: Just replace the name of the item in the array with a new string)
- Fletcher just remembered he's allergic to chocolate, so he decides to give you all the chocolate he's collected so far—Milky Way, Peanut M&M's, Three Musketeers, and a Hershey's bar! Isn't it great having friends like Fletcher around on Halloween?! (note: Add all of Fletcher's candy at once using only a single method)
- You can't wait any longer, so you go ahead and eat the M&M's.
- When you get home, you sort all of your remaining candy in alphabetical order.
- Now that it's all sorted, you count it and announce the final figure to your mom.
- Your mom asks what candy specifically, so you tell her (console.log) about all of them at once (single string with " and " in between each candy).

After you're done with this project (or before you're done if you're struggling with it), check to see how your answer compares with mine in the back of the book. Remember, there may be several ways to get a correct answer. It just needs to work with all of the different array changes and finish with the correct candy in the correct order.

LOOP A ROUND

In the last chapter, you learned five cool things about arrays (plus two more things that were kinda "meh")! In this chapter, you'll learn the most useful thing of all that you can do with an array. Now is a time of discovery. Now you will learn...the loop!

The Illustrious `while` Loop

No programming language would be complete without some way to **loop**. A loop in JavaScript (and in other programming languages) is a block of code that will repeat itself over and over again as long as some **condition** remains true. The condition is anything that you want the program to check before each and every time it loops. Whenever the condition is truthy, the program knows to repeat. Once that condition is no longer truthy (i.e., it's falsy), then it's time to stop repeating.

Basic `while`

Here's a simplified example of a `while` loop (open a new blank Chrome tab and try this out in the console):

```
let counter = 0;
while (counter < 10) {
    console.log('counter is at ' + counter + ".  Let's add 1 to it.");
    counter++;  // the ++ incrementer is the same as `counter = counter + 1;`
}
console.log('Stop counting!');
```

So what's happening here? Well, first I'd like to ask you: "Can you figure it out just by reading the code?" If so, that's awesome! If not, don't worry; I'll break it down for you.
- The `counter` in this example starts at 0.
- The *condition* for the while loop (the part in parens) states that this block of code should be repeated over and over as long as (i.e., "while") the `counter` is less than 10.

- Because the initial value of `0` is less than `10`, we run this block of code.
- Each time the block of code is run, the interpreter goes back up to the top and checks the condition again. If the condition is still truthy, the code will be run again (that's why we call this a "loop").
- Inside this block of code, we increase the value of the `counter` by `1`. This is important because without this incrementer, the `counter` would stay at `0`. Then the condition (`counter < 10`) would *always* remain true and the code would continue to loop forever! (Note: If you accidentally do that at some point, you may need to restart your Chrome browser to get it to stop so you can begin working again).
- Because the `counter` keeps getting increased by 1 in every loop, eventually (after 10 loops), the `counter` will equal `10`.
- After that happens, the interpreter will check the condition (`counter < 10`) and see that it now resolves to false. At this point, the interpreter will quit looping and move on to the final line of our code.

Following Conventions

Now I'll write the same piece of code but I'll change the variable name from `counter` to `i`.

```
let i = 0;
while (i < 10) {
    console.log('i is at ' + i);
    i++;
}
console.log('Stop counting!');
```

Okay, so what was the point of that? Was it necessary to change the variable name? Not at all. So why do it? While it's true that there's nothing special about the variable name `i`, a good reason to use it is simply that it is common practice among software developers to use the lowercase letter `i` as a variable name to represent something that counts up or down in a loop. When a decision or style is not required, but it is a common accepted practice in the industry, we call this a coding **convention**.

Many of the things I've taught you in this book so far are not actual requirements but rather are done *by convention*. One example of this is camelCase variables. Your programs will still work if you write your variables in UPPERCASE, lowercase, or snake_case. But by following the *convention* of writing in camelCase, your code will look more similar to that of professionals, and other developers will have an easier time reading and understanding it.

So as I mentioned above, it is by convention that we use the letter `i` as the incrementer to count up (using the `++` increment operator) or down (using the `--` decrement operator) in a loop. If you continue with your software development career, you will see the variable `i` used for this purpose hundreds of times. I want you to be comfortable seeing it.

Real Life `while` Loop

Now here's how a **while** loop might apply to a real-life situation...

Suppose you're 3 years old. (You were 3 years old once, right?) You've been playing with building bricks all morning, but now your mom wants you to put them all back in the bucket. There are literally hundreds of these building blocks on the floor. You realize quickly that you couldn't possibly carry them all at once. So you do the only sensible thing you can think of: you start to cry. Just then, your mom, in all her brilliance, shows you an amazing trick for accomplishing this seemingly insurmountable task: pick up just a few of the building bricks at a time, put them in the bucket, then go back and do this again. You should keep doing this until all of the building bricks are off the floor and in the bucket.

You think through the plan...The math checks out! This just might work! Let's break down the various facets of your mom's plan:

- Assume that you have **const**antly found your `brickCarryingCapacity` (the number of building bricks you can hold at one time) to be about 10 bricks.
- let us also assume that there are `230` building `bricksOnTheFloor`.
- The instructions are to grab all the bricks you can carry and remove them from the floor (i.e., subtract your `brickCarryingCapacity` from the total of `bricksOnTheFloor`).
- `while` there are any building bricks left on the floor (i.e. as long as this *condition* remains true), you need to keep repeating (i.e., "looping") those same instructions.

Here's how the plan might be drawn up using JavaScript:

```
const brickCarryingCapacity = 10;
let bricksOnTheFloor = 230;
console.log('There are ' + bricksOnTheFloor + ' bricks on the floor.');
while (bricksOnTheFloor > 0) {
    // augmented assignment (from ch. 2): `x -= y;` is the same as `x = x - y;`
    bricksOnTheFloor -= brickCarryingCapacity;
    console.log('After putting away ' + brickCarryingCapacity
        + ' bricks, I now have ' + bricksOnTheFloor + ' bricks left.');
}
console.log('Hooray!  All the bricks have been put away!');
```

Did you follow all that? Now here's something cool about that loop: You could do it with any number of `bricksOnTheFloor`, and it would be pretty much the same amount of code! To make it more flexible, we're going to turn this into a function that accepts one parameter. If you think you can do this on your own, please try it out. If not, then type along with me.

First press the **UP_ARROW** in the console to bring back the code, then wrap it in a named function call like this:

```
function cleanUpBuildingBricks() {
    // ... (the code from above goes here)
}
```

Then remove the `bricksOnTheFloor` line and instead add `bricksOnTheFloor` as a new parameter inside the parens. When you're done, your function should look like this:

```
function cleanUpBuildingBricks(bricksOnTheFloor) {
    const brickCarryingCapacity = 10;
    console.log('There are ' + bricksOnTheFloor + ' bricks on the floor.');
    while (bricksOnTheFloor > 0) {
        bricksOnTheFloor -= brickCarryingCapacity;
        console.log('After putting away ' + brickCarryingCapacity
            + ' bricks, I now have ' + bricksOnTheFloor + ' bricks left.');
    }
    console.log('Hooray!  All the bricks have been put away!');
}
```

Now you can call the function by simply "passing in an argument" (remember, an *argument* is passed into a function and its value is assigned to that function's *parameter*). The argument is a number that will become the new `bricksOnTheFloor` like so:

```
cleanUpBuildingBricks(400);
cleanUpBuildingBricks(30);
cleanUpBuildingBricks(1020);
```

See how that works? Now before moving on, I'll pose a little challenge for you: What if your `brickCarryingCapacity` wasn't a constant value? Can you think of a way to add an additional parameter to the function so that it accepts *two* numbers (separated by a comma)? The two numbers should become the `bricksOnTheFloor` and `brickCarryingCapacity` respectively. I think you can probably do that one on your own, so I'll leave you to it (refer to Chapter 4 if you need help).

The Famous `for` Loop

When creating our first `while` loop in this chapter, remember how we included that `counter` variable? I told you that it's really important that you remember to keep adding to the `counter` variable (we used a `++` **increment operator** to do this) in the body of the loop. If you forget to add to the `counter` variable, the program could get stuck in the loop forever, right?

Well, this situation is such a common occurrence with `while` loops that the JavaScript inventors created a close relative of the `while` loop for just such occasions. It's called the `for` loop. It's like a `while` loop with a built-in `counter` variable!

`for` **Loop Syntax**

The syntax for the `for` loop looks a little odd when you first see it. But take the time to learn it anyway because you may see this exact syntax thousands of times in your coding career. Type this in the console of a new blank Chrome tab:

```
for (let i = 0; i < 10; i++) {
    console.log('i is at ' + i);
}
console.log('Stop counting!');
```

Did that seem familiar to you? It should have. This is basically the exact same process that I used when introducing the `while` loop, but it's been shortened into a `for` loop! The three parts of the `for` loop are separated by semicolons. Each part was also in the `while` loop but in a different place. Let's examine each.

```
> let i = 0;
  while (i < 10) {
      console.log('i is at ' + i);
      i++;
  }
  console.log('Stop counting!');
```

initialize counting variable
condition to check
incrementer

```
> for (let i = 0; i < 10; i++) {
      console.log('i is at ' + i);
  }
  console.log('Stop counting!');
```

1. First we initialized the counting variable.

2. Next we included the condition that will be checked before every **iteration** of the loop (to determine if we should run the code block again). An iteration simply means a single pass through of the looped code block (i.e., if we loop 10 times, then the code has undergone 10 iterations).

3. The third part is the incrementer (or decrementer). This piece of code is run at the *end* of each iteration to ensure that our counting variable continues to change.

Practice `for` Loops

Pretty much any time you know how many looping iterations you wish to perform, you will want to use a `for` loop instead of a `while` loop. Because `for` loops are very common (considerably more common than `while` loops actually), I want you to have a lot of practice creating the syntax. Write code for each of these scenarios (pretend situations) in a new console window. Feel free to try these on your own or work along with me.

Loop Scenario: Run Laps

Your gym teacher, Mr. Payne, tells you to run 5 laps around the gym counting each out loud.

```
function runLaps(totalLaps) {
    for (let i = 0; i < totalLaps; i++) {
        console.log('Lap ' + i + '!');
    }
}
runLaps(5); // pass in the 5 as an argument to become totalLaps
```

Hmm..."Lap 0"? That doesn't seem right...Let's fix this so it has the correct number for each lap. But how? Well, think it through. Instead of "Lap 0" on the first iteration, we want it to say "Lap 1", right? And on the second iteration, we want it to say "Lap 2" (instead of "Lap 1").

So what's the pattern here? In each case, we want to display a number that is exactly 1 more than the variable `i`. Well we can do that with a simple `i + 1`. Once you clearly articulate (describe) what it is that you want, it suddenly seems easy! Update the inside of the function as follows:

```
    for (let i = 0; i < totalLaps; i++) {
        console.log('Lap ' + (i +  1) + '!');
    }
```

Uh oh...The next day, Mr. Payne is in a bad mood. Now he wants everyone to run 8 laps! Good thing we did this in a function! Now all we need to do is pass in the number 8 as the argument instead of the number 5!

```
runLaps(8); // next day
runLaps(10); // third day
runLaps(15); // fourth day (gosh!  your gym teacher is fierce!)
```

Loop Scenario: Monkeys on the Bed

There's some nursery rhyme that utilizes a decrementing (backward counting) `for` loop. I don't remember the exact details, but I'm pretty sure this is the gist of it: 10 monkeys continue to jump on a bed despite clear instructions from their doctor. Each monkey in turn falls off, prompting their somewhat negligent mother to seek medical attention.

```
function monkeysOnBed(totalMonkeys) {
    for (let i = totalMonkeys; i > 0; i--) {
        console.log(i + " little monkeys jumpin' on the bed.  "
            + 'One fell off and suffered a mild concussion.');
    }
    console.log('The badly injured monkeys declined further comment.');
}
monkeysOnBed(10);
```

Loop Scenario: Powerball Lottery

Your town lottery has instituted a new Powerball lottery game. They need you to generate 6 random numbers between 1 and 20. Note: This will use the built-in `Math.random()` and `Math.floor()` functions introduced in chapter 4. Refer back to that chapter if you need a refresher on how these work together.

```
function getPowerballNumbers(totalLotteryPositions, minValue, maxValue) {
    for (let i = 0; i < totalLotteryPositions; i++) {
        console.log(Math.floor(Math.random() * maxValue) + minValue);
    }
}
getPowerballNumbers(6, 1, 20);
getPowerballNumbers(6, 1, 20); // should be a different set of 6 numbers
getPowerballNumbers(7, 1, 20); // different set of 7 numbers now
```

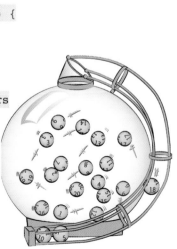

Loop Scenario: Count Very High

You have asked your dad too many times today if you can have a bowl of ice cream. Now, as a stall tactic, he has ordered you to count all the numbers from 1 to 300 before you're allowed to ask him for ice cream again (note: This one will use an array!).

```
function countEm(highestNumber) {
    const allTheNumbers = []; // initialize empty array
    for (let i = 0; i < highestNumber; i++) {
        allTheNumbers.push(i + 1); // add 1, 2, 3... etc. to the
array
    }
    console.log(allTheNumbers.join(', '));
    console.log('... NOW may I have some ice cream?');
}
countEm(300);
countEm(500);
countEm(1000); // Okay! Okay! You can have some ice cream! (Sheesh!)
```

Looping Through Arrays

At the beginning of this chapter, I promised to show you the coolest thing (or maybe I said "most useful thing" or something like that...) that you can do with arrays. But first, you had to learn about how loops work in order to understand it. Well, now that you've learned about loops *and* arrays, you will discover that these two programming concepts were practically made for each other! It's like I've taught you how to spread peanut butter and how to spread jelly separately, but now...IT'S PEANUT BUTTER JELLY TIME!

And you know what else is cool about this? From now until the end of the chapter, I'm not even going to teach you anything new! I'm only going to use the things you already know and show you how to put them together in useful ways. Let's get started!

Array with a `while` Loop

We'll look at the less common one first: the `while` loop. We will create an array of the steps you need to take to play your new video game: Yourscraft (now with Story Mode!). Then we'll use the `while` loop to make sure each step has been done. Go ahead and close all of your programs, then get to the console of a blank Chrome tab and type this:

```
let stepsToPlay = [
    'Plug the TV into the wall',
    'Plug the ZCrate One Z console into the wall',
    'Plug the HDMI cable into both the TV and the ZCrate',
    'Turn on the TV',
    'Turn on the ZCrate',
    'Click the Yourscraft icon',
    'Play the game (watch out for exploding stalkers!)'
];
```

So the goal is to use a `while` loop to print off each one of these items on its own line in the console. Knowing what you've learned in the last chapter and this one so far, it's possible you'll be able to do this without any further instructions (hint: remember the `.shift()` method from the last chapter). If you think you can do this on your own, go ahead and try it now! If you're not ready yet, then read on and we'll do it together.

We want to begin by logging to the console the first item of the `stepsToPlay` array. We can do this in one of two ways (don't type these yet, just read them):

```
stepsToPlay[0];  // returns first item (array is unchanged)
stepsToPlay.shift();  // returns first item (and REMOVES it from the array!)
```

Because the second option actually *changes* the number of items in the array (removing the first item each time it's called), we can put this in a loop and there will be a different item coming out during each iteration.

But remember: whenever you're working with any loop, you need be extra careful that it doesn't repeat forever! You need to have a condition that you know will not *always* remain true. And we can do that by checking the array's length. If the array loses an item every time, then the `.length` of the array will keep getting smaller until it's at 0. Try this:

```
while (stepsToPlay.length > 0) {
    const nextStep = stepsToPlay.shift();
    console.log(nextStep);
}
```

If you did that correctly, all of the steps should've been printed out to the console! And another thing—let's see how many steps we have left:

```
stepsToPlay;
```

An empty array. Because the while loop kept removing items from the array, we don't have any left to look at.

But I'd like us to do this again and make some minor adjustments. So press the **UP_ARROW** about 3 times or so until you get the initialized array again (the one that starts with `let stepsToPlay = [`). Then remove the `let` keyword. As you may recall, this now means that we're *changing* this variable instead of creating it brand new. Now run that code (press the **ENTER** key) to change the array to have all the original steps again.

Now let's simplify the `while` loop a bit. Try out this new `while` loop (it should behave exactly the same way), and then compare the changes to the old version:

```
while (stepsToPlay.length) { // old way had (stepsToPlay.length > 0)
    console.log(stepsToPlay.shift()); // old way had an extra variable
}
```

Does it seem strange to you that we removed the "> 0" from the condition? Think about it this way: `stepsToPlay.length` returns the number of items in the array. That number of items is always a positive integer—unless it's the number zero—right? Well every possible integer (whole number) is truthy...with *one* exception. You guessed it! Zero!

As long as the number of items in the array is not zero, then the condition is truthy, and the `while` loop will continue to run. As soon as the number of items drops to zero, then the condition is falsy (0 is a falsy value, remember?), so we break out of the `while` loop.

As for middle part (inside the `while` loop), all we did there was combine two lines into one. Because `stepsToPlay.shift()` returns a string, we can immediately `log` it to the `console`. Remember that whenever a function is called *inside* of another function, the interpreter will evaluate the functions from the inside out—i.e., the inner function will be run first!

Array with a `for` Loop

As I mentioned before, `for` loops are even more popular than `while` loops. In this next example, we're going to loop through an array using a `for` loop. And unlike our `while` loop example above, we are going to do this without actually changing the array itself.

```
const cookieSteps = [
    'Preheat oven to 350 degrees',
    'Mix margarine, sugar, brown sugar, vanilla, and eggs',
    'Mix flour, cornstarch, salt, baking soda, and chocolate chips',
    'Place dough on cookie sheet',
    'Cook for 12 minutes',
    'Remove cookies from oven',
    'Eat cookies!'
];

for (let i = 0; i < cookieSteps.length; i++) {
    const stepNumber = i + 1; // 1st step will be "Step 1" instead of "Step 0";
    const thisStep = cookieSteps[i];
    console.log(stepNumber + '. ' + thisStep);
}
```

Full disclosure: I've never made cookies in my life. But I got this recipe from my daughter, and she makes delicious cookies!

Were you able to understand why that works? As the code gets looped over and over, the value of `i` increases by 1 on each iteration. So in the first pass through, the value of `i` is `0`. Now we know that `cookieSteps[0]` returns 'Preheat oven to 350 degrees' right? Well since `i` represents `0` in the first pass through, `cookieSteps[i]` will return the same value as `cookieSteps[0]`.

Then on the second pass through, the value of i is the number 1, and on the third pass through, the value of `i` is `2`, etc. So `cookieSteps[i]` ends up being the same as typing `cookieSteps[1]`, `cookieSteps[2]`, and so on with each iteration. Get it?

And because our `for` loop doesn't state the exact number of times it needs to repeat, we can add to or subtract from the array all we like, and it will still work just fine!

159

```
cookieSteps.push('Pour yourself two quarts of milk');
cookieSteps.push('Finish eating every last cookie');
cookieSteps.push('Feel guilty for not sharing any with your sister');
cookieSteps.push('Get a tummy ache');

for (let i = 0; i < cookieSteps.length; i++) { // slightly simplified; still works
    console.log((i + 1) + '. ' + cookieSteps[i]);
}
```

And check this out! We can do something more to simplify this code even further and still get it to return the exact same information. I probably wouldn't write it this way in my own code, but I'm going to do this here because I want you to be comfortable seeing how `for` loops work. Compare this code block to the one we wrote before and see if you can spot all the changes (note: We don't have to reset the array this time because we never actually changed the array when we used the `for` loop).

```
for (let k = 1; k <= cookieSteps.length; k++) {
    console.log(k + '. ' + cookieSteps[k - 1]);
}
```

Did you spot all the differences? Here are the ones I most want you to notice:

1. We used a `k` instead of an `i`. No reason other than to show you that there's nothing uniquely special about `i`. It works with any other variable name as well.

2. We changed the initializer to `k = 1;` instead of `k = 0;` (or `i = 0;`). That means the value of `k` will go `1-7` instead of `0-6`. Again, in most of my code, I would start with 0. I just want you to know you can start with `1`—or any other value—if needed.

3. We changed the `<` to `<=`. This is important if we are starting with `1`. Otherwise, we would break out of the loop without getting to the last array item.

4. We used `cookieSteps[k - 1]`. Maybe you can guess why we did this. Because our `k` starts with 1, we need to subtract 1 from it at this point or else we would be starting with `cookieSteps[1]` ("Mix margarine, sugar, brown sugar, vanilla, and eggs"). If we did that, we would never get around to preheating the oven, and we would end up eating unbaked cookie dough. Hmm...actually...that doesn't sound too bad!

So here's the big takeaway: Arrays and loops (especially `for` loops) go together all the time in multiple programming languages. Learn the syntax and start thinking of using arrays any time you have a *list* of something. And use `for` loops almost any time you want to do something with each item of the list. If you structure your `for` loops correctly, then you get the freedom to alter your list however you—or your users—see fit, and your code will still work as intended.

Follow Along: Movie Spoilerator

Stella is one of your more eccentric friends. She loves watching movies, but she sometimes gets the endings mixed up in her head. This causes embarrassment for her at parties. Lucky for her, Stella has a good friend who has promised to make for her a movie ending generator to help her remember...and as you probably guessed, that friend is you.

You agreed to create a function that will allow Stella to type in a movie title and return back that movie's ending...*sigh*...How do you get yourself talked into these things?

Oh well. What kind of friend would I be if I didn't at least try to help you? So you want my advice? Here's the plan: you're going to make two lists (hint: Whenever you hear the word "list," you should think "array"). One list will have the titles of several well-known movies while the other will contain a short description of the endings of each of these movies. It is important that the two lists be in the same order (e.g., the third movie on the first list should correspond with the third ending on the other list).

```
const movieTitles = [
    'Annie',
    'Shrek',
    'Toy Story',
    'Star Wars',
    'Frozen',
    'Hamlet',
    'Cinderella'
];

const movieEndings = [
    'Mr. Warbucks adopts Annie.',
    'Fiona stays an ogre.',
    "Buzz accepts that he's a toy.",
    'The Death Star is destroyed.',
    'Elsa stops ruining everything.',
    'Everybody dies.',
    'They all live happily ever after.'
];
```

Now wrap both of these arrays in one function (hint: Either use the **UP_ARROW** in the console to bring back your lists or copy/paste them). This function should have one parameter (i.e., it expects one argument to be passed in) and that will be the title of the movie that the user wishes to have spoiled. Include the //TODO: comments too:

```
function getMovieSpoiler(chosenMovie) {
    // ... (your arrays go here now)

    //TODO: logic will go here soon
    //TODO: your return statement will go here
}
```

Okay now. Just to make sure that the function is working properly, put a `return` statement at the bottom of the function in place of the last //TODO: comment (just above the final closing curly brace). Assume that your user called this function without passing in a proper movie title, or maybe one that's not on the list or something. What should the function `return` in that case? Perhaps something exciting and witty like this:

```
    return "Sorry, we don't have that movie on our list.";
```

Go ahead and test out your function:

```
getMovieSpoiler('Fake Movie Title'); // No surprise there.
getMovieSpoiler('Annie'); // Huh?  But I was almost sure...
getMovieSpoiler('Toy Story'); // Wait a minute...
```

So the function should work...ish. The problem is that it always `returns` the same message. Now press the **UP_ARROW** in the console a few times to bring back the function and make edits on it. You can now add in the logic to compare the movie title against your list of titles and return the correct spoiler. By the way, remember to press **SHIFT+ENTER** if you need to make new lines inside the function).

Important: You must include this logic piece above the existing `return` statement. This is because as soon as the JavaScript interpreter executes (runs) a `return` statement in your code, it will jump out of the function and not read anything else inside the function after that. So, *above* the `return` statement (in place of the remaining `//TODO:` comment), type:

```
for (let i = 0; i < movieTitles.length; i++) {
    if (movieTitles[i] === chosenMovie) {
        return movieEndings[i];
    }
}
```

Now look at that code block carefully. It's not easy (at this stage in the book, you are past the point of easy coding), but it does make sense and it uses only things you've already learned so far. Can you figure out the logic? Do you know why it works?

If you've done everything correctly so far, your function should look something like this:

```
> function getMovieSpoiler(chosenMovie) {
      const movieTitles = ['Annie', 'Shrek', 'Toy Story', 'Star Wars', 'Frozen', 'Hamlet', 'Cinderella'];
      const movieEndings = ['Mr. Warbucks adopts Annie.', 'Fiona stays an ogre.', "Buzz accepts that he's a toy.", 'The
  Death Star is destroyed.', 'Elsa stops ruining everything.', 'Everybody dies.', 'They all live happily ever after.'];

      for (let i = 0; i < movieTitles.length; i++) {
          if (movieTitles[i] === chosenMovie) {
              return movieEndings[i];
          }
      }

      return "Sorry, we don't have that movie in our list.";
  }
```

Try it out a few times to be sure the function works as expected:

```
getMovieSpoiler('Annie'); // Much better.
getMovieSpoiler('Hamlet'); // Oh, how sad.  :-(
getMovieSpoiler('Cinderella'); // Hooray!  :-)
```

On a high level, your function is looping through all of the items in the `movieTitles` list and comparing them to the `chosenMovie` parameter. If it finds a match, it runs a `return` statement returning the `movieEnding` that exists at the same index point as the matching `movieTitle` (that's why the same variable i is used). And once a `return` statement is executed, no other code is run after that, so you never get to the final `return` statement saying, "Sorry, we don't have that movie..." Get it?

Now this is good enough to put a fork in it and call it done. But sometimes we developers like to add a little extra pizazz...

Suppose instead of just being able to call this with a single movie, Stella wants a function where she can pass in a *list* of movies and get the spoilers back for each. Now keep in mind that you should not make any changes to the existing function. You will create a *new* function that calls the existing one (perhaps multiple times inside of a loop). If you think you might be able to do this on your own, please try before reading on.

Still with me? Okay, here's the code for one possible solution. Type it in the console and verify that it works:

```
function spoilTheseMovies(listOfChosenMovies) {
    console.log('SPOILER ALERT!  Here are the endings of some famous movies...');
    for (let i = 0; i < listOfChosenMovies.length; i++) {
        const movie = listOfChosenMovies[i];
        console.log(movie + ': ' + getMovieSpoiler(movie));
    }
}

spoilTheseMovies(['Toy Story', 'Frozen', 'Hotel Rwanda', 'Annie']);
spoilTheseMovies(['Star Wars', 'Shrek', 'Boring Talking Movie for Grown-Ups']);
```

Now assuming you got it to work, don't stop there. Look back at it carefully. Play with it and change it if you like. See if you can figure out on your own why it works. Don't just copy working code. Dissect it until you understand it. Learning to read and understand code when you see it is a huge part of being a professional software engineer...the other huge part is looking up stuff in Google. (That probably sounds like a joke, but every engineer I know will tell you it's true.)

CHAPTER 9: QUIZ

Do the whole quiz in your Workbook without looking back at the chapter. After you're finished, have a parent check your answers against the back of the book (or check them yourself if no parent is available).

1.   What is the term for a block of code that will repeat itself over and over again as long as some condition remains truthy?

2.   What word could you put in the blank space in this block of code?
```
let i = 0;
_____ (i < 5) {
    console.log(i);
    i++;
```

3.   Of the two kinds of loops that we discussed in this chapter, which is more commonly used for arrays?

4. Your code may get trapped in a never-ending _____ if the _____ always remains truthy.

5. How many individual messages (lines) will be logged to the console using this code?
```
const countyNums = [1, 2, 3, 5, 6];
for (let j = 0; j < countyNums.length; j++) {
    console.log(j + ' => ' + countyNums[j]);
}
```

6. When a decision or style is not required, but it is a common accepted practice in the industry, we call this a coding _____.

7. How many individual messages (lines) will be logged to the console using this code?
```
let k = 0;
while (k < 7) {
    console.log('line!');
```

8. What character is used to separate each of the three sections inside the parens of a `for` loop?

9. Of the three sections inside the parens of a `for` loop, what is the middle section called?

10. Will any message(s) be logged to the console as a result of running this code? If not, why not? If so, what will be logged to the console? (Answer *before* testing it out!)
```
const top40Hits = ['Hey Jude', 'Billie Jean', 'Imagine', 'Hotel Calif.'];
for (let m = 1; m <= top40Hits.length; m++) {
    if (top40Hits[m] === 'The Chicken Dance') {
        console.log('Excellent choice!');
    } else if (top40Hits[m] === undefined) {
        console.log('Big mistake.');
    } else if (top40Hits[m] === 'Hey Jude') {
        console.log("Oh hey! Didn't see ya there!");
    }
}
```

11. How many individual messages (lines) will be logged to the console using this code?
```
const maxCounter = 17;
let n = 0;
while (n <= maxCounter) {
    console.log('count it! ' + n);
    n++;
}
```

12. What word refers to a single pass through of a looped code block?

13. What should you put in the blank space in this block of code?
```
const hats = ['cowboy', 'bowler', 'chef', 'top'];
for (let p = 0; p < _____; p++) {
    console.log('I like to wear a ' + hats[p] + ' hat.');
}
```

CHAPTER 9: **KEY CONCEPTS**

Read this list and look back in the chapter to review anything you're not solid on before moving on:

- Loop
- `while` loop
- Condition
- Coding conventions
- `for` loop
- Iterations
- Incrementer in a `for` loop
- Arrays with `while` loop
- Arrays with `for` loop
- Calling a function within a loop

CHAPTER 9: **DRILLS**

A. Try typing these valid code snippets in the console

As you type the comparisons into the console, ask yourself what exactly you expect the value to be. Then look at the response from the console to see if you're correct.

1.
```
let i = 0;
while (i < 6) {
    console.log(i);
    i++;
}
```

2.
```
const sevens = [];
for (let i = 0; i < 10; i++) {
    sevens.push(i * 7);
}
sevens.join('|');
```

3.
```
while (sevens.length) {
    console.log(sevens.shift());
}
```

4.
```
for (let j = 0; j < 20; j++) {
    if (j % 2) {
        console.log(j + ' is an odd number.');
    } else {
        console.log(j + ' is an even number.');
    }
}
```

5.
```
const letters = 'abcdefghijklmnopqrstuvwxyz'.toUpperCase().split('');
const backwardAlphabet = []; // initialize empty array
```

```
    for (let k = letters.length; k > 0; k--) { // counting down (not up)
        backwardAlphabet.push(letters[k - 1]); // add letter to array
    }
    backwardAlphabet;
```

6.
```
const vowels = 'aeiou'.toUpperCase().split(''); // create array of vowels
while (backwardAlphabet.length) { // keep looping till other array is empty
    const thisLetter = backwardAlphabet.pop(); // remove letter from array
    for (let m = 0; m < vowels.length; m++) { // loop through the 5 vowels
        if (vowels[m] === thisLetter) { // check if this letter is a vowel
            console.log(thisLetter + ' is a vowel.');
        }
    }
}
```

7.
```
for (let i = 0; i < 30; i+= 3) {
    console.log(i);
}
```

8.
```
function whichNumbersAreDivisible(maxNumber, divisor) {
    console.log('Which numbers less than ' + maxNumber
        + ' are divisible by ' + divisor + '?');
    for (let n = 0; n < maxNumber; n++) {
        if (!(n % divisor)) {
            console.log(n + ' is divisible by ' + divisor + '!');
        }
    }
}
```

9.
```
whichNumbersAreDivisible(100, 10);
```

10.
```
whichNumbersAreDivisible(60, 5);
```

11.
```
whichNumbersAreDivisible(90, 3);
```

12.
```
let p = 0;
while (p < 52) {
    console.log(p);
    p += 5;
}
```

13.
```
function multiplicationChartLine(baseNumber) {
    const chartColumns = [];
    for (let i = 1; i <= 10; i++) {
        chartColumns.push(baseNumber * i);
    }
    return chartColumns.join(' | ');
}
```

14.
```
multiplicationChartLine(3);
```

15.
```
multiplicationChartLine(5);
```

16.
```
multiplicationChartLine(7);
```

17.
```
function fullMultiplicationChart(baseNumber) {
    const chartRows = [];
    for (let i = 1; i <= baseNumber; i++) {
        chartRows.push(multiplicationChartLine(i));
    }
}
```

```
        return chartRows.join('\n');
    }
```

18.   `fullMultiplicationChart(2);`

19.   `fullMultiplicationChart(6);`

20.   `fullMultiplicationChart(10);`

B. What's wrong with each of these code snippets?

1.
```
while (let i = 0; i < 6; i++) {
    console.log(i);
}
```

2.
```
let q = 10;
for (q > 0) {
    console.log(q--);
}
```

3.
```
let trafficLightColors = 'red-yellow-green'.split('-');
for (const r = 0; r < trafficLightColors.length; r++) {
    console.log(trafficLightColors[r]);
}
```

4.
```
function getAllTheRainbowColors() {
    const colors = 'red,orange,yellow,green,blue,indigo,violet'.split();
    for (let i = 0; i < colors.length; i++) {
        console.log('one of the colors is: ' + colors[i]);
    }
    console.log("And that's all the colors of the rainbow!");
}
getAllTheRainbowColors();
```

5.
```
function countByTwos() {
    for (let r = 0; r <= 10; r+= 2) {
        return console.log(r);
    }
}
```

6.
```
function countByTwos() {
    for (let s = 0; s <= 10; s++) {
        if (s % 2) {
            console.log(s);
        }
    }
}
```

CHAPTER 9: **AGGREGATE REVIEW**

This is the last Aggregate Review for the whole book! I know it's super long, but look at it this way: almost every question represents a different thing that you've learned over the course of this book (and of course there are many more things not listed). Look at everything you've learned! Isn't that amazing?! If you've gotten this far, you're amazing too! You're in the home stretch now with this final aggregate review. Make it count!

1.   The _____ operators we use are `===`, `!==`, `>`, `>=`, `<`, and `<=`.

2.   A value that isn't necessarily a boolean, but is treated as `true` for the purpose of conditional statements is said to be generally _____. If it were treated as `false` (though not a boolean), it is said to be generally _____.

3.   True/False: Logical operators always result in a boolean value.

4.   What does DRY stand for in coding?

5.   True/False: When there are functions nested inside of one another, the interpreter will always evaluate the functions *from the inside out* (i.e. process the results of the values for the inner functions before processing those for the outer functions).

6.   What code might you use to get a random integer between `0` and `40`?

7.   What does the .length of an array refer to? What does `.length` of a string refer to?

8.   Does this appear to accomplish the developer's intention? (And if not, why not?)
`const hoursInADay = 24;`

9.   The _____ in an array is the number representing any given item's position in the array.

10.   True/False: Block comments cause the JavaScript interpreter to ignore everything from the first `/*` until the next `/*`.

11.   What built-in method can you use to add a new item to the end of an array?

12.   What is the name for the primitive data type that means no value has been assigned?

13.   What glossary term refers to the practice of repeatedly calling one method after another on an object, in one continuous line of code?

14.   By convention, most developers use what form of capitalization for function names in JavaScript?

15.   True/False: Calling `myArray.join('\n')` on an array will return a string with a newline

character (a.k.a. break return) between each item of `myArray`.

16. Is this a valid block of code? (And if not, why not?)

```
const tonightsBand = 'Three Wheels of Cheese';
tonightsBand = "Sal Monella and the Disease"; // TWoC couldn't make it
```

17. What code should go in the blanks to generate a random value from the array?

```
const coldPlacesToLive = ['Antarctica', 'the North Pole', 'Canada'];
const randomIndex = Math._____(Math._____() * coldPlacesToLive._____);
const coldPlace = coldPlacesToLive[randomIndex];
console.log('You should have a warm coat if you live in ' + coldPlace);
```

18. What is a developer trying to arrive at when she uses modulo in an operation?

19. Answer this before testing it out in the console: what will be the result of this code?

```
['Z', 'Y', 'W', 'X'].toString().toLowerCase().split(',').sort()[1];
```

20. What's the value of `mobileDevice` after this line?

```
const mobileDevice = 'phone' || ('tablet' && 'PDA');
```

21. What's the value of `nonMobileDevice` after this line?

```
const nonMobileDevice = 'TV' && ('laptop' || 'Desktop');
```

22. What are two different ways to shorten (simplify) this line of code?

```
opponentsScore = opponentsScore + 1;
```

23. Which mathematical operator would be most useful for checking if a given value is evenly divisible by 5?

24. True/False: Error messages are intended to be human-readable so that developers can have clues to help in resolving the errors.

25. Which comparison operator returns `false` if the value on the right is less than or equal to the value on the left?

26. True/False: After running this code, the trainCars array will have a .length of 5.

```
const trainCars = ['engine', 'freight car'];
trainCars.push(['passenger car', 'baggage car', 'caboose']);
```

27. What built-in function can you use to round a float (number with a decimal point) down to the nearest integer (number without a decimal point)?

28. What does a single equals sign imply in a statement?

29. What key combination can you press to get a break return (new line) in the console?

30. True/False: The `alert()`, `confirm()`, and `prompt()` functions are often avoided because they block all code from running until the user responds.

31. True/False: The `confirm()` function always returns a boolean.

32. What are the three keywords that may be used to declare a new variable? Which keyword will you probably use most of the time? Which one might you never use?

33. Your code may get trapped in a never-ending _____ if the _____ always remains truthy.

34. What do you type in order to create a new line in the console (note: this also works with any plain text formats such as alert(), confirm(), and prompt() messages)?

35. When a decision or style is not required, but it is a common accepted practice in the industry, we call this a coding _____.

36. Similar to the comparison operators, the _____ operators (&&, ||, and !) work well in conditional statements.

37. What word refers to a single pass through of a looped code block?

38. Is this valid code (feel free to type it in the console)? (And if not, why not?)
```
function hasEnoughMoneyToBuy(walletMoney) {
    const cost = 10.30;
   if (walletMoney > cost) {
     console.log('You have enough money!');
   } else {
     console.log("You can't afford it!");
   }
}
hasEnoughMoneyToBuy(10.30);
```

39. How many individual messages (lines) will be logged to the console using this code?
```
let x = 10;
while (x > 0) {
   console.log('value of x is ' + x);
   x++;
}
```

40. Is this valid JavaScript? (And if not, why not?)
```
function fixThePrecisionTo3Decimals(number) {
   return number;
   const preciseNumber = number.toFixed(3);
   console.log('More precise amount = $' + preciseNumber);
   return preciseNumber;
}
fixThePrecisionTo3Decimals(25.98765);
```

41. How many individual messages (lines) will be logged to the console using this code?
```
const colors = ['red', 'orange', 'yellow', 'green', 'blue', 'purple'];
for (let i = 0; i < colors.length; i++) {
   const color = colors [i];
   if (color.length >= 5) {
      console.log(color);
   }
}
```

42. True/False: !!('clever' && 'handsome'); // (from my personal profile)

43. What glossary term refers to code that has helpfully-named variables and descriptive function names so that it's easy for a developer to understand the purpose of the code as he reads it (without the need for explanatory comments)?

44. What is the symbol for the logical operator that always returns a boolean (when placed before a falsy value, it returns true; before a truthy value, it returns false)?

45. True/False: Comparison operators always result in a boolean value.

46. The values `null`, `false`, `''`, 0, and `undefined` are all _____; whereas `true`, `'string'`, and `1` are all _____ values.

DIY: Strange Allergies

Your doctor just called. The test results are in. I hate to break it to you, but you have a very unusual food allergy. It turns out you are allergic to all candy bars whose names end in the letter "s". And here you were just about to sit down and enjoy all the candy that you got while you were out trick-or-treating (your DIY from the last chapter)!

For this DIY project, I'd like for you to loop through the list of candy from the previous chapter and log messages regarding the safety of eating each piece of candy. As a reminder, your list of candy includes: Butterfinger, Hershey's, Kit-Kat, Milky Way, Peanut M&M's, Snickers, Starburst and Three Musketeers. Create a custom function that will log 8 separate messages (one for each piece) stating whether or not you may eat each given piece of candy from this list. As always, you may refer to my solution in the back if you get stuck.

10 MAKE A HANGMAN GAME

You have come such a long way to get here! Everything you have learned in this book is specific to the JavaScript language, but most of it applies to many other programming languages as well. By that, I mean that in addition to JavaScript, you have already built the foundations for learning how to program in Ruby, Python, PHP, Java, C#, and many other languages that are used in famous websites and powerful companies around the world. You are well on your way to having the skills you need to make an awesome career.

Up to this point, you've been working hard and learning new things in each chapter. Now the learning is done. You've earned a break! I'd like us to have a little fun together. So in this, the final chapter, I will not teach *anything* new. Instead, we'll use many of the concepts you've *already* learned and put them together to create something cool: a Hangman game!

Have you ever played Hangman before? It's a game that is often played between friends on a bus ride or something. Here's the basic concept: The game picks a random word from a word bank. It's the player's goal to guess that word by picking individual letters from the alphabet. But with every wrong guess, the player gets closer to losing the game (and hanging the innocent man!). Can the player guess the whole word before it's too late?!

I'm going to explain my thought process through every single step, so you should be able to follow along with me to create this game yourself. I also show the full, complete code in the Answers section in the back of the book, so if you ever get lost, you can compare your code to mine and fix any bugs you see. If there is any piece of this you don't fully understand while I'm writing, just do your best to copy it down correctly as it may make more sense after you see the completed game.

But remember this: Every single line of this whole game uses concepts we have already discussed in this book—no exceptions! I hope as you work through this with me, you'll start to get a glimpse of the awesome new powers that are available at your fingertips. I mean think about it: how many of your friends would be able to build a working video game from scratch and actually understand every single line of code in it?! You are amazing!

Setup

Most of the work you've done so far has been directly in the console. You can build this entire game in the console too if you like (the final game will run there), but I actually recommend you write your code in your Workbook (or any text editor if you prefer). When this game is finished, there will be around 85 lines of code. I think you'll find it easier if you can type it in your Workbook, so that it is easy to make changes and fixes as you go along.

Several times, I'll have you test out your code in the JavaScript console. When it's time for that, I'd like you to simply copy and paste your code into the console. You're probably familiar with copy/pasting at this point (see Chapter 1), but if not, here's a refresher:

1. Use your mouse to highlight the lines of code in your Workbook.
2. Copy the lines of code with **CONTROL+C** (or **COMMAND+C** on a Mac).
3. Paste the code inside the console with **CONTROL+V** (or **COMMAND+V** on a Mac).

One important word of warning though: when copying your code from your Workbook, it is crucial that you followed the directions from Chapter 1 and turned OFF "smart quotes" in your Google Docs or Microsoft Word preferences. Smart quotes are turned *on* by default in both of these programs, but your code will not work unless you turned that setting *off*.

Okay, that's enough setup I think. You ready to get started? Let's have some fun!

Create the Goal: `generateHangmanSolution()`

In this game, we'll create three separate functions (which are, as always, named following the same camelCase conventions we've been using since Chapter 1). You should be able to call them all individually to make sure they work in the console. The first function will generate a Hangman solution for you. Go ahead and type all this in your Workbook or text editor, then copy/paste it into your console to test it out.

```javascript
function generateHangmanSolution() {
    const possibleSolutions = [
        'watermelon',
        'volleyball',
        'homecoming',
        'strawberry',
        'retirement',
        'television',
        'friendship',
        'cinderella',
        'restaurant',
        'helicopter',
        'skateboard',
        'leadership',
        'antarctica'
    ];
    const randomIndex = Math.floor(Math.random() * possibleSolutions.length);

    return possibleSolutions[randomIndex].toUpperCase();
}
```

If you copied all of this properly, this function should select a random word from the supplied word bank and that word should be in all capital letters. Example responses might be: "HELICOPTER", "STRAWBERRY", "VOLLEYBALL", etc. Test it out in the console:

```
generateHangmanSolution();
generateHangmanSolution();
generateHangmanSolution();
```

Hopefully, most of this function already makes sense to you. I'm going to explain it to you now, but before I do, I'd like you to look it over and see if perhaps you can figure out every line on your own. If you can, that's even better! If you need some help though, don't sweat it. This is meant to be fun after all. Just do your best to follow my explanations, okay?

- For the first part of this function (beginning with `const possibleSolutions`), create a simple array of possible words. I've included 13 possible words here, and they're all 10 letters long. There's nothing special about these. You don't have to use any of them if you don't want to. I actually recommend you add many more words to this list. Use any words you like, but ideally they should be common and kinda long.
- For the second part (beginning with `const randomIndex`) generate a random integer between 0 and 12 (all the possible valid indexes for the array). As we saw in Chapter 8, if we put any of those numbers in square brackets after the array name, we'll be sure that we are getting a value that exists in the array (e.g., `possibleSolutions[1]` would give us `'volleyball'`).
- For the last part (`return` statement), grab a random value from the array using the `randomIndex` and convert that value `toUpperCase()` before `return`ing it. Easy peasy.

Skip to the End: `gameOver()`

Now we're going to jump straight to the end! We'll create a `gameOver` function that should give our user (the player) a message. When creating a game, I think it's a very good practice to create the ending before fleshing out the middle. The reason for this is that as you create the game, you have a clear end goal in mind, and you can continue to test that your code is working properly at each intermediate step. Without this end goal, you'll end up writing a lot more code before testing it. Then when you finally do test it out and it doesn't work as expected (code almost *never* works correctly the first time), there'll be so many lines of code at once that it may become hard to identify where the bugs are.

So here's the code. Most of this function should be easy to understand. The part I'll explain first though is the `asciiHangman` line. That is just a tiny piece of ASCII art (art created using characters on your keyboard). It's like the teddy bear we created in Chapter 4. You don't have to memorize it or anything. Just type it out carefully and you'll see the little picture it creates. Type this function in your Workbook, then copy/paste it into the console:

```
function gameOver(solution, won) {
    const asciiHangman = '_____\n|/  |\n|   @\n|  /|\\\n|  / \\\n|\n=====';
    let message = '';
    if (won) { // if `won` parameter is missing, this will be falsy (undefined)
        message = 'YOU WIN!';
    } else {
        message = 'GAME OVER\n\n' + asciiHangman;
    }
    message += '\n\nThe correct answer was ' + solution + '!';
    alert(message);
    return message;
}
```

This is a function that expects up to two parameters. The first parameter, `solution`, is the correct solution to the puzzle. The second parameter, `won`, is a boolean value stating whether the player has won or lost. As you may recall from Chapter 4, if you call the function without passing in two arguments, then any parameters that don't get a value will automatically have the value of `undefined`. And because `undefined` is a falsy value, it will behave the same as passing in `false`! Let's test this out in the console:

```
gameOver('WATERMELON', true); // YOU WIN!
gameOver('ANTARCTICA', false); // GAME OVER
gameOver('FLUFFYBUNNIES'); // GAME OVER
const tempSolution = generateHangmanSolution();
gameOver(tempSolution, true); // YOU WIN!
gameOver(tempSolution); // GAME OVER
gameOver(generateHangmanSolution(), true); // YOU WIN!
gameOver(generateHangmanSolution()); // GAME OVER
```

Time to break it down!

- I already explained the first line (about the ASCII art).
- In the next 7 lines, create the `message` to be displayed to the user. If the function is invoked passing in `true` for the `won` parameter, the first line of the `message` will be positive (`"YOU WIN!"`). Otherwise, it's negative (`"GAME OVER"` plus the hangman art).
- Because the second part of the `message` is the same regardless of whether the player won or lost, we use an *augmented assignment* (Remember from Chapter 2?) to add the rest of the `message`. Also, note that the `\n` creates a newline character, which helps in our formatting.
- For the remaining two lines, simply `alert()` this `message` and then `return` it. You might be asking yourself: "Why are we using `alert()`? Didn't Jeremy say that users find it annoying?" Well, truth be told, we will be using all three of the functions I told you that users find annoying: `alert()`, `confirm()`, and `prompt()`. I wouldn't ordinarily use these myself, but I was determined to create this whole game using only the techniques I've taught so far in this book. And these three functions are the only methods of user-interaction I've taught you so far, so that's why we're using them. In my next book, I plan to teach you some more elegant options, and you can use those from that point on.

The Main Function: `playHangman()`

Now we come to the main event. For this section, I'll show you a little at a time, and we'll keep working our way to the end. At the end of each subsection, you should be able to run the main function without any errors (even if it's unwinnable initially). Pay attention to this kind of workflow as it is one that you'll want to use in your own projects in the future.

Structure

Type this function in your Workbook then copy/paste it into the console. Be sure to actually type out all of the `//TODO:` comments as these will help you when we add more code to know exactly where it needs to be added.

```
function playHangman() {
    const solution = generateHangmanSolution();

    //TODO: add other initialization variables here

    //TODO: add confirmation message here

    //TODO: add game loop here

    return gameOver(solution, false); // if player gets here, Game Over (fail)
}
```

This is the scaffolding (the structure) for our main game. Right now, all it does is what you were doing manually earlier:

- Generate a `solution`.
- Then invoke the `gameOver` function passing that `solution` in as the first argument.

You should be able to test it out right now by invoking this function in the console:

```
playHangman();
```

Note that it is error-free right now. If you add something later and it causes an error for you, try backtracking to the latest point when you knew it was working. Continually test your code like this and you'll save yourself time and headaches!

Variables

Now type this in your Workbook or text editor in place of the `//TODO: add other initialization variables here` comment:

```
    const solutionLetters = solution.split('');
    const wrongGuesses = [];
    const maxWrongGuesses = 7;
    const progressSoFar = '_'.repeat(solution.length).split('');
```

Once you've done that, then highlight the whole `playHangman()` function in your Workbook (from the word `function` to the final closing curly brace) and copy/paste it in your console. Here's an explanation of each line in order:

- Generate the `solution` to the game and store the string to an unchangeable variable.
- Create an array of individual characters (we will use this later when we capture the player's letter guesses).
- Make an empty array to store the player's wrongly guessed letters.
- Decide how many `wrongGuesses` (strikes) the player gets before he's out. Feel free to adjust this up or down to reduce or increase difficulty.
- Create an array of underscores (_) that has exactly as many items as there are characters in the `solution` word (if you haven't added any of your own words yet, then we know this will be 10 items in length because all the possible solutions are 10 characters long). This is what the player starts with. We intend to change each of these underscores to correctly guessed letters as the game progresses.

And just to be on the safe side, go ahead and test that the function works without errors:

```
playHangman();
```

Troubleshooting

Hopefully, that function worked properly and without any errors... But what if it didn't? What if you got an unexpected error? Or worse: what if you didn't get any errors, but the code didn't execute as you expected? Well, if that's the case, you'll need to do some **troubleshooting** (looking for the cause of a problem and fixing it).

To begin with, if you got an error message, try to use that to fix the problem (that's the easiest solution most of the time). If that's not enough, compare each line of your code to the lines in the book. Also, make sure that your quote marks and apostrophes are not "smart quotes" or "smart apostrophes" (i.e. they should not curl one way or the other).

You might also try putting chunks of your code in comments to make sure that the rest of it runs properly. Get the simplest version of running code that you can. Then, one by one, start adding in the commented lines (i.e. uncomment the lines) and testing the code several times along the way. You do this to make sure that the code still runs properly. Eventually, you'll add in a line or two, and the code will not run. When that happens, that will tell you to look extra carefully at that line. Hope this helps you troubleshoot! If your code works properly now, remember this section and refer back to it if you need it in the future.

Confirmation

Now in your Workbook, in place of the `//TODO: add confirmation message here` comment, put this block of code:

```
const confirmPlay = confirm("Let's play Hangman!\n\n"
    + "Pick letters to guess the word I'm thinking of.\n"
```

```
            + "It's a common word with " + solution.length + ' letters.\n'
            + 'Are you ready to play?');
    if (!confirmPlay) {
        return gameOver(solution, false);
    }
```

Here are our goals for each of these lines:

- Invoke a `confirm()` dialog box asking the user if he wants to play. As you may recall from Chapter 7, `confirm()` requires the user to click a button (either "OK" or "Cancel") and will `return` either `true` or `false` accordingly. We take this `return` value (`true` or `false`) and assign it to a variable so that we can test for it next.
- In this `if` statement, check if the user confirmed (`true` or `false`). You may remember from Chapter 6 that when there's a `!` in front of it, it will resolve the opposite. So it will run the code inside the curly braces only `if` the user clicked the "Cancel" button.
- If the user clicked "Cancel," send him straight to the `gameOver` function and pass in `false` for the second argument. This means that the user did not win, so they'll get the "GAME OVER" message without success. (Note: This will work just as well if you leave out the second argument so it would look like `return gameOver(solution);`.)

Once again, copy the entire `playHangman()` function from your Workbook and paste it in the console. Now try it out—fix any error messages if you see them—and click the "Cancel" button when you're offered the `confirm()`:

```
playHangman();
playHangman();
```

If you're curious, you might have also tried clicking the "OK" button on the `confirm()` message. If you did that, then the interpreter would've skipped over the first `if` block, but you still would've gotten the failing `gameOver` message at the bottom. That's only because we haven't written the rest of the game yet. Don't worry about that.

At this point, we've established what will happen if the user clicks "Cancel," so you might be expecting an `else` block to show what happens if the user *doesn't* cancel. It might surprise you to know that the `else` block is actually unnecessary here. Why is that? Because of the `return` statement we've already written! If the condition inside the `if` block were to resolve true, then the `return` statement would be run, and *nothing else inside a function can happen after running a `return` statement*. Therefore, everything we write after this block can *only* be run if the `if` statement resolves `false`! So there's no need for an `else` block! It behaves the same as if all the rest of the code in the function were already inside a giant `else` block. This isn't new information, but it may be looking at old information in a new way.

The Game Loop

There's something interesting to know about pretty much all video games: They're written to run in a loop. The game shows the player some situation, then takes her input (key presses, button presses, etc.), then changes the situation based on that input (sometimes only slightly) and accepts her input again. The loop continues to run—perhaps thousands or millions of times—until some condition causes the end to happen. Perhaps, the player runs out of lives (Game Over) or perhaps she gets all the stars and wins or perhaps she just decides to quit playing. Either way, the same pattern is there: loop loop loop until something breaks the cycle.

CAUTION: INFINITE LOOP

Knowing that concept should help you a lot in understanding how to write this or any other game. So let me break down for you what we're trying to accomplish in *our* game loop:

1.   Set up the loop to continue as long as the player hasn't made too many wrong guesses (`wrongGuesses.length < maxWrongGuesses`). Check this condition at the start of every loop and kick the player out of the loop if need be.
2.   Show the player his `progressSoFar` (e.g. "_ _ _ _ _ _ _ _ _ _", or "S T _ _ W B _ _ _ _", etc.).
3.   Show the player his `wrongGuesses` (so he doesn't guess them again).
4.   Ask the player to pick a letter.
     a. If he cancels, exit the loop and send him to `gameOver` (failure).
     b. If he submits a letter, continue on...

We'll get to the rest later. But let's write the code for that much first. Type this part in your Workbook in place of the `//TODO: add game loop here` comment:

```
while (wrongGuesses.length < maxWrongGuesses) {
    const promptMessage = 'Here is your progress on the word so far: \n'
        + progressSoFar.join(' ') + '\n'
        + 'Wrong Guesses: [' + wrongGuesses.toString() + ']\n\n'
        + 'Pick a letter!';
    const userInput = prompt(promptMessage);

    if (!userInput) {
        return gameOver(solution);
    }

    //TODO: process user's guess here
}
```

Now copy/paste the `playHangman()` function into your console to test it. It's not possible to win yet, but it shouldn't get stuck in an infinite loop either. You should be able to exit at any time by pressing the "Cancel" button or submitting an empty string at the `prompt()`.

```
playHangman();
```

So we've now created a `promptMessage` by simply concatenating several strings the same way we've been doing since in Chapter 3. Then we passed in the `promptMessage` string variable to the built-in `prompt()` function that will be shown to the user at the start of each loop iteration. If the user cancels or enters an empty string, we kick him out of the loop and into the `gameOver` function with another `return` statement!

Does this make sense so far? If it doesn't, I recommend you continue on until the whole project is done and you've had the chance to try the code. Sometimes the big picture can seem a little fuzzy with all these details. When you have tested out the game a few times, come back and read this stuff again, and it will probably make much more sense to you.

So what's next in our loop?

5. Collect the letter that the player submits and assign that to the variable `guess`.
6. Check if the solution has that letter (`guess`) in it.

    a. As long as there is at least one match, make a note that his `guess` was correct (it doesn't add to his `wrongGuesses`).

    b. For each matched letter, update the `progressSoFar` to include the `guess`.

We'll do the rest soon. But for now, put this code in place of the `//TODO: process user's guess here` comment in your Workbook:

```
const guess = userInput.toUpperCase();
let goodGuess = false;

for (let i = 0; i < solutionLetters.length; i++) {
    if (solutionLetters[i] === guess) {
        goodGuess = true;
        progressSoFar[i] = guess;
    }
}

//TODO: Add logic for right or wrong guess here
```

Most of this should be fairly readable to you now. Here are the steps:

*   Convert the player's input `toUpperCase()` and assigned it to the `guess` variable.
*   Create a new boolean variable (using `let` since it will be changeable) called `goodGuess` and give it the default value of `false` (we'll make it `true` later if we find the player's `guess` is in the solution word).
*   After that, use a `for` loop (as seen in Chapter 9) to loop through each of the letters of the solution word and compare it to the player's `guess`.

    *   If any one letter matches the `guess`, change the `goodGuess` variable to true and also update the `progressSoFar` array so that the item in that position will no longer be an underscore ("_") but will instead be that guessed letter!

For example, suppose the solution is "STRAWBERRY" and the `progressSoFar` array is ['S', 'T', '_', '_', 'W', 'B', '_', '_', '_', '_']. If the player's `guess` is "R", then this code will loop through every character of "STRAWBERRY" (the solution) in order, comparing it to the `guess`. When it finds a match at position 2 (the variable `i` will represent the number 2 at that point), it will run `progressSoFar[2] = "R"`. The same will happen for the other two appropriate positions: `progressSoFar[7] = "R"` and `progressSoFar[8] = "R"`. When this code block is done, the `progressSoFar` array will be ['S', 'T', 'R', '_', 'W', 'B', '_', 'R', 'R', '_'].

You should be able to test out what you have so far—even though the game is still unwinnable. Try this out and see if it shows progress when you guess letters.

`playHangman();`

Did that kinda work? No error messages? Okay, so what comes

next? Well, we have that `goodGuess` variable that was initialized as `false`. If there were any letter matches, it would be `true` at this point. So let's test it and react accordingly. Here's what we want to do:

7.   Check the `goodGuess` boolean to see if the player's `guess` was correct.
       a. If `true`:
            i. Check to see if he has completely solved the puzzle.
                 • If he has, `return` successful `gameOver` (`"YOU WIN!"`).
                 • Otherwise, continue on...
            ii. `alert()` the player that his `guess` was right.
       b. If `false`:
            i. Add the player's `guess` to the array of `wrongGuesses`.
            ii. `alert()` the player that his `guess` was wrong, and tell him how many strikes he has left.

So let's see what this looks like in code. Put this block of code in place of the `//TODO: Add logic for right or wrong guess here` comment in your Workbook:

```
if (goodGuess) {
    if (progressSoFar.join('') === solution) {
        return gameOver(solution, true);
    }

    alert('Good guess!');
} else {
    wrongGuesses.push(guess);
    alert('Sorry, ' + guess + ' is incorrect.\nYou have '
        + (maxWrongGuesses - wrongGuesses.length) + ' strikes left.');
}
```

See if you can read and understand this on your own. I think you can, but just in case, I'll explain the lines here. (Might as well be thorough, right?) I hope this feels repetitive to you because that implies that you have a good understanding of how to read code!

- If `goodGuess` is `true`...
    ○ Open another `if` statement to compare the `solution` to our `progressSoFar` array. Because we're comparing a string to an array, we use the `.join()` method and pass in an empty string so that it will combine each of the array items into a string of characters with no other strings in between them.
        • If this is a perfect match, run a `return` statement, which of course will boot our player out of this whole `playHangman` function (not running any further code here) and into the `gameOver` function. But this time, pass in `true` as the second argument. When the `gameOver` function reads this, it will execute the `"YOU WIN!"` version of the `message` (refer to the `gameOver` function declaration to see what I mean).
        • If this is not a match, continue on...
    ○ `alert()` the player that his `guess` was a `"Good guess!"`.
- If `goodGuess` is `false`...
    ○ `.push()` the `guess` into the `wrongGuesses` array. Remember that `wrongGuesses.length` will be compared against `maxWrongGuesses` (using the "less than" comparative operator

discussed in Chapter 5) before every iteration of this `while` loop. If the `.length` is ever too high, the player will be forced out of the `while` loop which will lead him to the final `return gameOver()` statement (FAILURE).

- ◦ `alert()` the player that his `guess` was incorrect and show how many strikes he has remaining before the [presumably] innocent man will be hanged.

And that, my friends, was the FINAL block of code for the whole game! Copy/paste all of your code in the console and test it out as many times as you like!

```
playHangman(); // try to reach all of the possible outcomes!
playHangman(); // try solving the puzzle!
playHangman(); // try canceling at the start!
playHangman(); // try running out of guesses!
playHangman(); // try canceling partway through it!
playHangman(); // test it out with a parent or sibling!
```

Improvements

At this point, your Hangman game should completely work. If it doesn't work properly, try out some of the error resolution steps we explored in Chapter 1. If that doesn't help, then check the Answers section in the back of the book because I put the full solution in there. Compare your code to mine line-by-line to see if there's any section that is missing or doesn't add up.

If you have gotten it to work, congratulations! Next, I encourage you to look back through the code to ensure that you fully understand every single line. The code touches on many different concepts that were first introduced in every chapter leading up to this point! I actually didn't even plan that! It just worked out that way because programming languages continue to build upon themselves much like spoken languages do (think about it: just today, you probably used words you first learned at every different year of your life!).

If you have a working Hangman game and you understand the code, feel free to call it done! Or if you're still eager for more, consider making minor improvements to the game on your own. Perhaps you'd like to try some of these ideas?
- Add a dozen or more words to the solutions word bank.
- Change the text presented to the player.
- Add helpful comments to explain the code more fully.
- Add in the Hangman ASCII art in other places.
- Create your own ASCII art to be displayed when the player wins.
- Adjust the input collection to elegantly handle situations where the player inputs more than one character (perhaps only use the first letter of his input?).
- Anything else you can think of...

This Hangman game is all yours now, so however you wish to use it is up to you! Have fun exploring!

Conclusion

I hope you've enjoyed this small introduction to your newfound abilities. But even more, I hope you'll continue to expand them and improve your skills. All of this volume has focused on JavaScript, and that's a great foundation for learning to code. But a balanced programmer should also know a little bit about some other languages too. This is just the beginning. There is so much more that you can do!

For instance, did you notice that in this whole book, we never displayed any actual images? You learned a ton about programming and creating functions, but we never did anything with colors. We didn't create a web page or embed a video or build something you could email to your friends. Is that because those concepts are too difficult? Absolutely not!

You can learn all of those things and so many more after that! The reason we didn't touch on any of them in this book is because they all fall into the subjects of HTML (Hypertext Markup Language) and CSS (Cascading Style Sheets). If you can learn JavaScript, you can *definitely* learn both of these skills as well! In fact, most developers agree that they are considerably *easier* to learn than JavaScript.

So if HTML and CSS are easier to learn, why didn't I start with them? Well, the truth is that I could've started with them. The development concepts that arise when studying HTML, CSS, and JavaScript all build on one another, and different people learn them at different times. I had a teaching approach with JavaScript that I was excited about exploring, so I started with that.

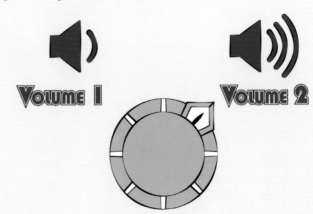

I wanted to help you learn to think through problems and create solutions like a real engineer. I wanted you to tap into the new skill of programming computers, and I believe JavaScript is the best place to start that new discovery.

But I still want you to learn HTML and CSS so that you can develop entire websites, involve your JavaScript in creative new ways, and build projects that will last!

That's why I strongly encourage you to check out Volume 2 of my *Code for Teens* series. In Volume 2, I'll introduce you to HTML and CSS and show you how JavaScript becomes *so* much cooler when you weave it in with these concepts. You'll build interactive web pages and games, manipulate images, and save and share your work with your family and friends! You can say goodbye that sad feeling of "Well, it was a cool project, but I did it all in the console, and I can't find it anymore..."

If you enjoyed this book, I guarantee you'll enjoy the sequel too! Either way though, do continue to learn and grow. Never stop improving. I hope you'll continue your journey of discovery and develop your superpowers beyond what you ever thought possible!

Answers

Chapter 1 Answers

Ch. 1 Quiz Answers:

1. `about:blank`
2. CONTROL+SHIFT+J
   (COMMAND+OPTION+J on a Mac)
3. `let` and `var`
4. `;`
5. `/`
6. paren (parens is the plural form)
7. SyntaxError (the `;` was unexpected there. It should've been moved to the right side of the closing paren).
8. camelCase (or camelCasing)
9. paren (would also accept quote mark)
10. Not valid because the `let` keyword should not be there in the second line.
11. Assignment—a value is being assigned to a variable (example: `let myAge = 10;`)

Ch. 1 Drills Answers:

A. Try typing these valid code snippets in the console

1. `"pepperoni and sausage"`
2. `21`
3. `4`
4. `12`
5. `14`
6. `"6 Foot 7 Foot"`
7. `Working 9 to 5"`
8. `"73"` // the "3" is a string so the 7 is concatenated (attached) to it instead of the value added to it.
9. `Infinity`

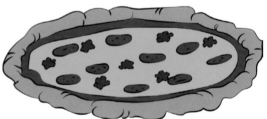

B. What's wrong with each of these code snippets?

1. Needs `var` or `let` keyword before using the variable.
2. Missing closing quote mark (`"`)

3. The single equals sign implies *assignment*. Assignments always need to have exactly one variable on the left side (like `let x = 3 + 5;`). Also, it needs the `let` or `var` keyword when declaring a variable for the first time.
4. SyntaxError. The semicolon is unexpected. The closing paren should come first.
5. Missing closing paren (or has extra opening paren)
6. Missing opening paren (or has extra closing paren)
7. The single equals sign implies *assignment*. Assignments always need to have exactly one variable on the left side (like `let x = 15 - 12;`). Also, it needs the `let` or `var` keyword when declaring a variable for the first time.
8. Missing semicolon (`;`) on the end (note: this will not actually throw an error)
9. The variable `notreallycamelcase` is in **lowercase**. It should instead be in camelCase like this: `notReallyCamelCase` (note: This is by convention; no error would be thrown here).
10. The variable `ISTHISANYBETTER` is in **UPPERCASE**. It should instead be in camelCase like this: `isThisAnyBetter`
11. The variable `how_about_this` is in **snake_case**. It should instead be in camelCase like this: `howAboutThis`.
12. The variable `IsThisCloseEnough` is in **PascalCase**. It should instead be in camelCase like this: `isThisCloseEnough` (lowercase letter to start the variable).
13. The variable `surely-this-counts-right` is in **kabob-case**. This is NOT valid JavaScript at all as the dashes would appear to the interpreter to be minus signs! It should instead be in camelCase like this: `surelyThisCountsRight`.
14. Missing quotes around the string `"Good!"` (and better to also end with a semicolon).

Ch. 1 Do It Yourself (DIY) Recommended Solution:

Here is one possible solution to the DIY Project (try copying/pasting this whole block into the console to see the final return value):

```
let ageOfDad = 36;
let ageOfMom = 36;
let ageOfAngel = 13;
let ageOfTony = 11;
let ageOfHarmony = 8;
let ageOfCharity = 7;
let ageOfChase = 5;
let ageOfSymphony = 0;
let sumOfAllAges = ageOfDad + ageOfMom + ageOfAngel + ageOfTony + ageOfHarmony
    + ageOfCharity + ageOfChase + ageOfSymphony;
let numberOfFamilyMembers = 8;
let averageAgeOfFamilyMembers = sumOfAllAges / numberOfFamilyMembers;
averageAgeOfFamilyMembers;
```

Chapter 2 Answers

Ch. 2 Quiz Answers:

1. Plus sign indicates addition—adding numbers together
2. `*`
3. Number
4. Forward slash indicates division—dividing one number by another number
5. Number
6. Parens—`(` and `)`
7. `*=` (`myVariable *= 2;`)
8. `%` (percent sign)
9. `myVariable++;` (increment operator)
10. `myVariable--;` (decrement operator)
11. `3 * (4 + 1);`
12. `2`
13. `-=` (`myValue -= 8;`)
14. 5 different values (`0`, `1`, `2`, `3`, or `4`).
15. Augmented assignments
16. Modulo (`%`). In this case, you would use `% 3` because there are only three different possible values you're looking for (red, green, or blue).

Ch. 2 Drills Answers:

A. Try typing these valid code snippets in the console

1. `16`
2. `5`
3. `4`
4. `6`
5. `20`
6. `7`
7. `2`
8. `2`
9. `0`
10. `18` // note: this is one way to get the shortened 2-digit form of any given year
11. `3`
12. `1`

B. What's wrong with each of these code snippets?

1. In JavaScript, math operations should never appear on the left side of a single equals sign (`=`) because that sign indicates that a value is being assigned.
2. A variable name cannot be a number (nor even start with a number!).

3. While this statement isn't technically invalid, it probably indicates a logical mistake on the part of the developer. She probably intended to write:
    `mySpecialValue = mySpecialValue + 6;` or even cleaner:
    `mySpecialValue += 6;` (both would arrive at the same result)

4. Missing closing paren

5. Variable assignment requires a single equals sign (`=`), not a double equals sign (`==`)

6. `modDividend` and `modDivisor` must both be defined before they can be used on the right side of an assignment statement.

7. Missing opening paren

8. `+*` isn't a valid operator (it doesn't make sense).

9. In JavaScript, math operations should never appear on the left side of a single equals sign (`=`) because that sign indicates that a value is being assigned. Besides that, even if the right side and left side were switched, `theFinalAnswer` would still need a `let` or `var` keyword in front of it.

10. A `+=` symbol cannot be used along with a `let` statement. The keyword `let` indicates that a new variable is being created. A `+=` symbol cannot be used at the time a variable is first being created because it can't be added to itself (as it's not yet been defined when the addition would need to take place).

11. Operations should never appear on the left side of an assignment statement (remember that `-=` does indicate that a value is being assigned to a variable).

12. This doesn't throw an error, but for practical purposes, `%` should usually only be used with integers (positive or negative whole numbers) and usually positive ones at that (or `0`). There are some cases where it would be useful outside of this, but these cases are rare.

13. `+/` isn't a valid operator (it doesn't make sense)

Ch. 2 Aggregate Review Answers:

1. camelCase (or camelCasing)
2. CONTROL+SHIFT+J (COMMAND+OPTION+J on a Mac)
3. No. A variable name cannot start with a number.
4. Yes
5. True. Error messages are there to help you figure out what went wrong so you can fix it. That's why you should read those error messages!
6. SyntaxError
7. `%` (modulo)
8. `about:blank`
9. `+=` (`mathyValue += 7;`)
10. Yes. Multiple statements may appear on one line if separated by semicolons (`;`).
11. Not valid because the `let` keyword should not be there in the second line.

Ch. 2 DIY Recommended Solution:

Here is one possible solution to the DIY Project (try typing these lines into the console and running them one-at-a-time to see the final return value):

```
let numberOfCourts = 4;
let studentId = 1;      // first studentId (we'll change this with each line)
studentId % numberOfCourts;          // any number modded by 4 will return a value between 0
```
and 3. In this case, it returns 1 (as in, court #1)
```
studentId = 2; studentId % numberOfCourts;       // 2 (court #2)
studentId = 3; studentId % numberOfCourts;       // 3 (court #3)
studentId = 4; studentId % numberOfCourts;       // 0 (court #0)
studentId = 5; studentId % numberOfCourts;       // 1
studentId = 6; studentId % numberOfCourts;       // 2
studentId = 7; studentId % numberOfCourts;       // 3
studentId = 8; studentId % numberOfCourts;       // 0
studentId = 9; studentId % numberOfCourts;       // 1
studentId = 10; studentId % numberOfCourts;      // 2
studentId = 11; studentId % numberOfCourts;      // 3
studentId = 12; studentId % numberOfCourts;      // 0
studentId = 13; studentId % numberOfCourts;      // 1
studentId = 14; studentId % numberOfCourts;      // 2
studentId = 15; studentId % numberOfCourts;      // 3
studentId = 16; studentId % numberOfCourts;      // 0
```

Chapter 3 Answers

Ch. 3 Quiz Answers:

1.   b. human
2.   String
3.   c. ignore
4.   //
5.   SHIFT+ENTER
6.   quotes (single quotes or double quotes)
7.   /*
8.   */
9.   False. It doesn't matter which quotes you use.
10. characters (though if you said "strings," you wouldn't technically be wrong either)
11. concatenation
12. Add a \ before the apostrophe: `'The name\'s Bond. James Bond.'`
13. Change the single quotes to double quotes: `"Here's looking at you, kid.";`

Ch. 3 Drills Answers:

A. Try typing these valid code snippets in the console

1.   (type in the console. nothing to see here)

2. (type in the console. nothing to see here)
3. (type in the console. nothing to see here)
4. `KitKat`
5. `"Are we there yet?"`
6. `"No."`
7. `"Are we there yet? Are we there yet? Are we there yet?"`
8. `"We'll get there when we get there."`
9. `"But Mom said, "We will be there before you know it"!"`
10. `"I also said, "Quit pestering your father from the back seat"!"`
11. `"But I'm sooooo tired, and I can't sleep with my head on the window."`
12. `"If you don't quit your whinin', I'm gonna stop this car!"`

B. What's wrong with each of these code snippets?

1. The line that should've defined the variable is commented out (so the interpreter will ignore it). This leads to a ReferenceError because we're trying to use a variable that isn't defined.
2. The block comment is never closed.
3. Needs to escape the apostrophe in `I'm` with a backslash (or use double quotes on the string).
4. This will not be read as a block comment at all because the `//` will cause the rest of the line to be ignored.
5. There is an extra `/` at the end.
6. There is an errant `*` that should really be a `+`.
7. The i should be in quotes: `'i'`.
8. The backslash is in the wrong place. It should be moved one character to the right: `"The " + "\"dogs\" out?"`.

Ch. 3 Aggregate Review Answers:

1. CONTROL+SHIFT+J (COMMAND+OPTION+J on a Mac)
2. Yes
3. Yes
4. `about:blank`
5. No. In JavaScript, operators should never appear on the left side of a single equals sign (=) because that sign indicates that a value is being assigned.
6. True. Error messages are your friends. They're there to help you figure out what went wrong so you can fix it. Read those error messages!
7.  ```
    let age = 12;
    age += 1;
    ```
8. In the console (in Chrome developer tools)
9. SyntaxError (using `let` with the same variable more than once)
10. Yes
11. internet browsers (or just browsers)
12. camelCase (or camelCasing)
13. Parens—(and)
14. String (notice the quotes)
    ```

15. String (notice the quotes)
16. Assignment (assigning to a variable)
17. ```
    let faveEntree = "Chicken";
    faceEntree += " Burrito";
    ```
18. Modulo (or mod)
19. Yes (though it won't do much good since a value is assigned to a variable that is never used).
20. No. `favePopcorn` is never defined (the defining code is commented out).

Ch. 3 DIY Recommended Solution:

Here is one possible solution to the DIY Project (try typing this into the console or copy/pasting the whole block if you have a digital version of this book):

```
/* Variables */
let name = 'Jeremy';
let hobby = 'musical theater';
let pet = 'none (more of a children person)';
let skill = 'playing chess';
let grade = 31; // (good thing grades don't keep counting every year)
let faveCartoonMovie = 'Tangled';
let pronoun = 'he'; // as opposed to 'she'
let possessivePronoun = 'his'; // as opposed to 'her'
/* Now we'll add everything to one paragraph */
let bio = 'Even though ' + name + ' is super famous, ' + pronoun
    + ' still finds time to hone ' + possessivePronoun + ' skill of '
    + skill + ' and relax with ' + possessivePronoun
    + ' lovable pet named "' + pet + '".  In ' + possessivePronoun
    + ' free time, ' + pronoun + ' enjoys ' + hobby + ', watching "'
    + faveCartoonMovie + '", and studying to be on the honor roll at '
    + possessivePronoun + ' school where ' + pronoun + ' is in the '
    + grade + 'th grade.';
bio; // should print a long paragraph
```

Chapter 4 Answers

Ch. 4 Quiz Answers:

1. Function
2. Curly braces { and }
3. invoking (or calling)
4. camelCase
5. `return`
6. parameters / arguments
7. D.R.Y. (Don't Repeat Yourself)
8. `alert()`
9. Comma ,
10. `console.log()`
11. Parens `()`
```

12.   0 and 1 (referring to `Math.random()`)
13.   `Math.floor()`
14.   True
15.   True
16.   False. It will use the `return value` (also known as the "result") from the inner function and pass it as an argument to the outer function.
17.   TAB
18.   \n

Ch. 4 Drills Answers:

A. Try typing these valid code snippets in the console

1.   (type in the console. nothing to see here)
2.   `"Sweltering with scattered snow flurries"`
3.   (type in the console. nothing to see here)
4.   `"The weather forecast says:`
     `cloudy with a chance of meatballs"`
5.   (type in the console. nothing to see here)
6.   `"Your name is Jeremy"` //your results may vary
7.   (type in the console. nothing to see here)
8.   `"You are 36, and you still enjoy playing Xbox One?"` //your results may vary
9.   (type in the console. nothing to see here)
10. `3` //any integer from 1 and 6; your results may vary
11. (type in the console. nothing to see here)
12. `You rolled 11! (5 & 6)` //your results may vary

B. What's wrong with each of these code snippets?

1.   Function declaration is needed.
2.   Curly braces are needed { }.
3.   Curly braces are needed { } instead of square brackets [ ].
4.   `console.log()` should've been the outer function with `areDonutsTasty()` passed in as the argument (since it will return a string that can be logged to the console).
5.   `Math.random()` should be the inner function nested inside of `Math.floor()` as the return value of `Math.random()` would then be passed in as the argument to the outer function `Math.floor()`. Also, the value would be guaranteed to be exactly 0 in that case as any return value from `Math.random()` would be rounded down to the nearest integer: 0.
6.   This…is just wrong. Users hate `alert()` messages and find them annoying.
7.   The `semicolon` cannot be inside of the `console.log()` function. It needs to be at the end of the statement.
8.   Needs parens after `getColor`.
9.   Needs a parameter called `restaurant` inside of the parens on the first line in order to use it in the return value.

Ch. 4 Aggregate Review Answers:

1. String
2. `let` and `var`
3. True
4. Yes
5. Add a backslash before the apostrophe in `Can't`.
6. False. It's the D.R.Y. principle (Don't Repeat Yourself).
7. No. Developer probably wants a single-line comment, so it should be `//` instead of `/*`. The `/*` indicates a block comment so it must be closed with `*/`.
8. Number
9. `//`
10. characters
11. `%`
12. False. It is fine to have double quotes inside of a string surrounded by double quotes as long as the developer uses backslash to escape the inner quote marks like so: `"The children sang \"Jesus Loves Me\""`.
13. The remainder (or modulus) [of a Euclidian division problem]
14. True
15. Green
16. Console
17. Yes
18. Modulo `%`
19. `+=` (`largeNumber += 19;`)
20. String
21. No. The function declaration cannot use a number to represent the parameter. It should have a variable name there instead (and variable names cannot start with a number).
22. Create a break return (new line)
23. TAB
24. No. The function declaration shows two parameters in the function: `min` and `maxNumber`. When being invoked, only one number is passed into the function as an argument, so this number will be used as the first parameter (`min`), which is never used in the body of the function. The second parameter (`maxNumber`) *is* used in the function, but it will have the value of `undefined`, which will not achieve the stated goal of an integer less than 20.
25. nested

Ch. 4 DIY Recommended Solution:

Here is one possible solution to the DIY Project (try typing this into the console):

```
/*
 Town Lottery!
*/
function getRandomTwoDigitNumber() {
    let maxNumber = 100; // guaranteed less than this
    let randomNumberWithDecimal = Math.random() * maxNumber;
    let roundedDownToNearestInteger = Math.floor(randomNumberWithDecimal);

    return roundedDownToNearestInteger;
}
function getLotteryNumbers() {
    let part1 = getRandomTwoDigitNumber();
    let part2 = getRandomTwoDigitNumber();
    let part3 = getRandomTwoDigitNumber();
    let winningNumbers = part1 + '-' + part2 + '-' + part3;

    console.log('Your winning lottery numbers are: ' + winningNumbers + '!');
}
// Should be different every time
getLotteryNumbers();
getLotteryNumbers();
getLotteryNumbers();
```

Chapter 5 Answers

Ch. 5 Quiz Answers:

1. Boolean
2. < ("less than")
3. False
4. !== ("not equals equals" or "bang equals equals")
5. == and !=
6. >= // the wording on this one was tricky
7. Conditional
8. truthy / falsy
9. else
10. True
11. True
12. False (else block has no parens)
13. False

Ch. 5 Drills Answers:

A. Try typing these valid code snippets in the console

1. false
2. undefined // code inside if block doesn't run
3. true
4. true

5.   `truthy`
6.   `true`
7.   `kinda confusing`
8.   `false`
9.   `"See why we don't use this?  Confusing!"`
10.   `false`
11.   `false`
12.   `false`
13.   `undefined` // code inside `if` block doesn't run
14.   (type in the console. nothing to see here)
15.   `301 is greater than 212`
16.   `155 is greater than -800`
17.   `Both numbers are equal!`
18.   `efg is larger than abcd`
19.   `Both numbers are equal!`

B. What's wrong with each of these code snippets?

1. It's not invalid, but it should account for the possibility of the two numbers being the same value. As it is written, the console would log that one of the numbers is smaller even if they're the same.
2. The `if` block needs parens.
3. The `else` block should not have parens.
4. Having two comparison operators in one statement probably doesn't accomplish a very meaningful check.
5. Should be `===`.
6. This is an assignment, so it should be `=`.
7. This is an assignment, so it should be `=`.

Ch. 5 Aggregate Review Answers:

1. False. Block comments cause the JavaScript interpreter to ignore everything from the start of the comment with `/*` until the close of the comment with `*/`.
2. Yes
3. Put a backslash before each of the quote marks that surround the word "Goodbye" like this `\"Goodbye\"`
4. Don't Repeat Yourself
5. Conditional
6. Yes
7. String
8. `/*` and `*/`
9. falsy / truthy
10. A modulo operation (looking for the remainder)
11. camelCase

12. True
13. SyntaxError
14. Remainder of an integer division problem
15. No. There is an extra closing paren.
16. False. Error messages are intended to make it easier to see what's wrong.
17. Assignment
18. CONTROL+SHIFT+J (COMMAND+OPTION+J on a Mac)
19. Yes, it's valid, but it won't give you the result you're looking for. The > should be changed to >=.
20. += // like this... `greeting += ', ' + firstName;`
21. Boolean
22. Yes, it's valid, but it won't do what the developer probably wants. None of the code after the `return` statement gets run. For this reason, `return` should be the last line of the function.
23. `about:blank`
24. browsers
25. `==` and `!=`
26. `<=` // this was a tricky question. Look again if you got it wrong.
27. TAB
28. Yes
29. nested
30. True
31. `Math.random()`

Ch. 5 DIY Recommended Solution:

Here is one possible solution to the DIY Project (try typing this into the console):

```
/*
 Children's Church!
*/
function isInAgeRange(currentAge) {
    let minimumAge = 6;
    let maximumAge = 13;
    if (currentAge < minimumAge) {
        console.log("You're too young for Children's Church.");
    } else {
        if (currentAge <= maximumAge) {
            console.log("You may attend Children's Church!");
        } else {
            console.log("You're too old for Children's Church.");
        }
    }
}


// Now let's test it out
isInAgeRange(5); // too young
isInAgeRange(15); // too old
isInAgeRange(9); // just right!
isInAgeRange(13); // just right!
```

Chapter 6 Answers

Ch. 6 Quiz Answers:

1. Undefined
2. logical
3. Null
4. `undefined, undefined`
5. Logical OR, `||`
6. 1 possible value (`null`)
7. False
8. `else if`
9. Logical NOT, `!`
10. True
11. Logical OR, `||`
12. True
13. False
14. True
15. Logical AND, `&&`
16. True
17. `undefined`
18. 1 possible value (`undefined`)
19. True
20. `true` (remember, `!` always returns a boolean)
21. Logical AND, `&&`
22. falsy / truthy
23. `"love"`

Ch. 6 Drills Answers:

A. Try typing these valid code snippets in the console

1. `false`
2. `true`
3. `B`
4. `0`
5. `C`
6. `C`
7. (type in the console. nothing to see here)
8. `Person1 is older and goes first.`
9. `Person2 is older and goes first.`
10. `Person1 is older and goes first.`
11. `No ages have been passed as arguments!`
12. `Both are the same age. Let's randomly decide Person1 (or Person2) goes first!`

13. `No ages have been passed as arguments!`
14. `Person2 is older and goes first.`
15. `Person2 is older and goes first.`
16. (type in the console. nothing to see here)
17. `His name is Justin Thyme.`
18. `His name is John Doe.`
19. `His name is Rusty Karr.`
20. `His name is John Doe.`

B. What's wrong with each of these code snippets?

1. It's not invalid, but the final `else` block could never be run. Also, the `console.log()` statement in the first `if` block is misleading because `anyArgument` would have to be truthy for that block to run.

2. The `else if` block needs parens.

3. This is an assignment (that's what the = implies). In an assignment, there should only be one variable on the left side of the = with no operators or logic on that side.

4. This is an assignment (that's what the = implies). In an assignment, there should only be one variable on the left side of the = with no operators or logic on that side.

5. This is an assignment (that's what the = implies). In an assignment, there should only be one variable on the left side of the = with no operators or logic on that side.

Ch. 6 Aggregate Review Answers:

1. Yes.
2. Boolean, string, null (or object if you prefer), number, string, undefined
3. A modulo operation (looking for the remainder)
4. characters
5. True
6. logical
7. comparison
8. Conditional
9. nested
10. Yes, it's valid, but it won't give you the result you're looking for. The `if` block should use `>=` and `<=` so as to include those exact heights instead of excluding them.
11. False. `!` always results in a boolean value, but `&&` and `||` often result in non-boolean values.
12. `+=` // like this... `currentScore += 10;`
13. Modulo (`%`)
14. They're all truthy. The data types in order are: string, number, boolean, number, string, string.

199

15. Yes, it's valid, but it won't do what the developer probably wants. None of the code after the `return` statement gets run. For this reason, `return` should be the last line of the function.
16. `< // ` this was a tricky question. look again if you got it wrong.
17. The console
18. Wednesday
19. **TAB**
20. False. Nested parens and functions should always be resolved *from the inside out* (i.e. always resolve values for the innermost parens first).
21. True
22. No. The function declaration cannot use a number to represent the parameter. It should have a variable name there instead (and variable names cannot start with a number).
23. `Math.floor()`
24. True
25. True
26. **SHIFT+ENTER**

Ch. 6 DIY Recommended Solution:

Here is one possible solution to the DIY Project (try typing this into the console):

```
/*
 Temple of Stripes
*/
function templeDoorMessage(biForcePieces, halitosisWand, masterKey, regKeys) {
    let totalBiForcePieces = 6;
    let minRegKeys = 10;
    let msg;


    if (!(biForcePieces >= totalBiForcePieces)) {
        let numberMissing = totalBiForcePieces - biForcePieces;
        msg = 'You need ' + numberMissing + ' more Bi-Force pieces to enter.';
    } else if (halitosisWand && (masterKey || regKeys >= minRegKeys)) {
        msg = 'You may enter the Temple of Stripes!';
    } else {
        // let helpfulMessage = 'Bring stew to the mageSquire in obscureTown.';
        let crypticMessage = "Come back when you're more prepared.";
        msg = 'You are not ready. ' + crypticMessage;
    }


    console.log(msg);
}


// Now let's test it out
templeDoorMessage(4, true, true); // missing pieces
templeDoorMessage(6, true, false, 9); // not ready
templeDoorMessage(6, false, true); // not ready
templeDoorMessage(6, true, false, 12); // you're in!
templeDoorMessage(6, true, true); // you're in!
```

Chapter 7 Answers

Note: All Ch. 7 DIY recommended solutions are at the end of the answers section.

Ch. 7 Quiz Answers:

1. True
2. `toUpperCase()`
3. `const`
4. Documentation
5. When you know that the value of a variable might change.
6. `confirm()`, `prompt()`, and `alert()`
7. Self-documenting
8. `toLowerCase()`
9. Never
10. False. It goes by a special name: "method".
11. `prompt()`
12. `const`
13. False. It always returns a string (or `null`).
14. True
15. False. They create a poor user experience and block the rest of the code from running. For these reasons, professionals don't often use these functions anymore.

Ch. 7 Drills Answers:

A. Try typing these valid code snippets in the console

1. `"3.8"`
2. `"usernamewithweirdcapitalization"`
3. `Money value is $1.60`
4. `undefined`
5. `It's great to see you again, Jeremy!` // your results may vary
6. `undefined`
7. `"19"`
8. `"OFFICIAL PATENT OFFICE OF THE U.S.A."`
9. `"should be initialized with the let keyword"`
10. `All the things have been cleaned!` // your results may vary
11. `Thank you for your purchase!` // your results may vary
12. `undefined`
13. `"Sure!  I'll shake your hand!"` // your results may vary
14. `"I think I'll keep my distance."` // your results may vary
15. `"I think I'll keep my distance."` // your results may vary
16. `"Sure!  I'll shake your hand!"` // your results may vary

B. What's wrong with each of these code snippets?

1. You can't use `const` with a value that will change. Use `let` instead.

2. It's not invalid, but it's better to use `const` for both of these variables (instead of `let` or `var`) because they're not going to change.

3. Should use `prompt()` instead of `confirm()` since it requires the user's typed input.

4. C'mon, `toCapitalized()` is not a built-in function. Should be `toUpperCase()`.

5. This is not technically invalid, but it's probably not a good time to use `toFixed()` because it's rounding out a precise value and claiming that it's getting an `"extraPreciseAngle"`. If you're launching a missile into space, you probably shouldn't round out your angles without decimal places like that.

6. This is not invalid, but it's a poor example of self-documenting code. It would be better to name the variables with names like `daysPerYear`, `daysInAWeek`, and `hoursPerDay`. That way, the code would be self-documenting and wouldn't need those single-line comments by it.

7. This should be a `confirm()` instead of a `prompt()` because it's asking for a simple confirmation with only two possible values.

Ch. 7 Aggregate Review Answers:

1. falsy / truthy
2. Put a backslash before the apostrophe in Can't (like this: `Can\'t`).
3. Don't Repeat Yourself
4. Yes
5. `(Math.random() * 20).toFixed(2);`
6. Yes (and it's self-documenting)
7. False. Block comments start with `/*` and continue (often over multiple lines) until the first occurrence of `*/`.
8. String
9. `undefined`
10. camelCase
11. True
12. No. If the value of the variable will change, you should use `let` instead of `const`.
13. The remainder
14. `"homework"` (when using `||`, the first truthy value will be used, ignoring the rest)
15. True
16. assignment // look it up in the glossary if you're not sure what this means
17. True
18. True
19. `const`, `let`, and `var` (but try not to ever use `var`)
20. `\n`
21. logical

22. No, it's not valid because the parameter to receive is called `childAge`, and this parameter is never used. Instead a variable called age is used but it has never been defined. If you change the `age` to `childAge`, then the code would be valid. However, even after you do that, the code would still not work exactly as intended because the > should be changed to >= in order to not turn away 5-year-olds (minimum age).

23. Yes, it's valid, but it won't do what the developer probably wants. None of the code after the `return` statement gets run. For this reason, `return` should be the last line of the function.

24. `about:blank`

25. browsers

26. False

27. Self-documenting

28. !

29. falsy / truthy

30. True

Ch. 7 DIY Recommended Solutions:

Here are possible solutions to each of the DIY projects. Remember, your results may vary.

DIY [Spam Email Formatter]:

```
function formatSpamEmail(emailMessage) {
    return emailMessage.toUpperCase();
}

// Now let's test it out
formatSpamEmail('I am in much urgently needing of your help!');
formatSpamEmail('There shall is 42$-million USD in bank account for withdraw.');
formatSpamEmail('Send fast 2000$ Western Union to split millions half with you!');
```

DIY [Temperature Converter (Fahrenheit to Celsius)]:

```
function convertFahrenheitToCelsius(fahrenheitTemp) {
    const conversionRatio = 1.8;
    const fahrenheitFreezingPoint = 32;

    return (fahrenheitTemp - fahrenheitFreezingPoint) / conversionRatio;
}

// Now let's test it out
convertFahrenheitToCelsius(100);
convertFahrenheitToCelsius(32);
convertFahrenheitToCelsius(212);
```

DIY [Did You Also Floss?]:

```
function confirmTeethBrushedAndFlossed() {
    if (confirm('Did you brush your teeth this morning?')) {
        if (confirm('Did you also floss?')) {
            return 'Dr. Sizors will see you now.';
        } else {
            return "Use this dental floss and come back when you're done.";
```

```
        }
    } else {
        return 'Go brush your teeth first.  You can use the sink over there.';
    }
}

// Now let's test it out
confirmTeethBrushed();
confirmTeethBrushed();
```

DIY [Exotic Soup Chef]:

```
function makeFancySoup() {
    const ingredient1 = prompt("What's the first ingredient?");
    const ingredient2 = prompt("What's the second ingredient?");

    return 'Here is your ' + ingredient1 + ', ' + ingredient2 + ', and '
        + prompt("What's the third ingredient?") + ' soup!';
}

// Now let's test it out
makeFancySoup();
makeFancySoup();
```

DIY [Tip Calculator (Variable Rate)]:

```
function calculateTip() {
    const totalMealCost = prompt('What is the total cost of your meal?');
    const tipPercentage = prompt('What percent would you like to tip?') / 100;
    const decimalPlaces = 2; // money is usually rounded to 2 decimal places
    const tipAmount = (totalMealCost * tipPercentage).toFixed(decimalPlaces);

    return 'Your tip amount comes to $' + tipAmount;
}

// Now let's test it out
calculateTip();
calculateTip();
```

DIY [Letter Grade Generator]:

```
function generateLetterGrade() {
    const percentCorrect = prompt('What percent did you get correct?');
    if (percentCorrect >= 90) {
        return 'A';
    } else if (percentCorrect >= 80) {
        return 'B';
    } else if (percentCorrect >= 70) {
        return 'C';
    } else if (percentCorrect >= 60) {
        return 'D';
    }

    return 'F'; // this will only be run if no other return statements were reached
}

// Now let's test it out
generateLetterGrade(); // use 80
generateLetterGrade(); // use 53
generateLetterGrade(); // use 62
```

Chapter 8 Answers

Ch. 8 Quiz Answers:

1. Array
2. Number of items in the array
3. index
4. `0`
5. True
6. `.push()`
7. False. The return value will be a string that includes all of the items separated by commas.
8. remove / return
9. False. The `textbooks` array will not be changed. It will still have a `.length` of 2.
10. chaining
11. `"thimble"`
12. True
13. `.shift()`
14. `"gel"`
15. False. The return value will be a string that includes all of the items from the original array separated by the string `" or "`.
16. `d`
17. True
18. `5` (because there are 5 characters in the word "boots")

Ch. 8 Drills Answers:

A. Try typing these valid code snippets in the console

1. `undefined`
2. `"wake up"`
3. `"Here's my routine so far: brush teeth then get dressed then shower."`
4. `4` // array length
5. `"shower"`

    `"brush teeth"`
6. `"make my own lunch"`
7. `4` // array length
8. `"I have 4 things to do in the morning."`
9. `"Don't forget to brush teeth!"`
10. `undefined`
11. My old morning routine included `"eat breakfast,shower,get dressed,brush teeth"` but now it's `"eat breakfast, shower, get dressed, brush teeth, get books, make bed, fix hair"`.
12. `"Head, Knees, Shoulders, and Toes"`
13. `"B-I-N-G-O"`
14. `"Baby Shark"`

B. What's wrong with each of these code snippets?

1. Use `nuts.length` instead of `nuts.size`.
2. You need `nuts[2]` to retrieve the third item (because indexes start at zero).
3. Should be `nuts.push('hazelnut');`
4. `nuts.pop()` will remove and return the last item in the array—'peanut', which is a string, not an array, so the `.length` will not give the result you're looking for (it will only show the number of characters in the string "peanut").
5. Should be `.unshift('brazil nut');`
6. `fullList` is a string, so the `.shift()` array method won't work on it.
7. `nuts.concat()` returns a NEW array. This array was never assigned to anything so it was lost. The `nuts` array has not changed, so it will not look any longer than before.
8. Should be `nuts.sort();`
9. All of this would be just fine if `nuts` had been initialized with the `let` keyword. Because it was initialized with `const`, that variable name cannot be reassigned.

Ch. 8 Aggregate Review Answers:

1. Yes.
2. Number, null (or object if you prefer), undefined, string, boolean
3. characters
4. `toUpperCase()`
5. logical
6. comparison
7. `const`
8. Conditional
9. nested
10. Yes it's valid!
11. False. `!` always results in a boolean value, but `&&` and `||` often result in non-boolean values.
12. `confirm()`, `prompt()`, and `alert()`
13. `++` or `+= 1;` // like this... `currentRound++;` or `currentRound += 1;`
14. Modulo (`%`)
15. Never
16. They're all truthy. The data types in order are: number, string, boolean, number, string, string
17. Yes, it's valid, but it won't do what the developer probably wants. None of the code after the first `return` statement gets run. For this reason, `return` should usually be the last line of the function (unless it's the `return` is inside of an `if` block).
18. `<` // this was a tricky question. look again if you got it wrong.
19. The console
20. Eyes
21. True
22. Chaining
23. TAB
24. `.length` // like this `['simple', 'array'].length;`

25. True
26. True
27. Yes. But the function declaration receives a parameter and then does nothing with it. It would be better for this function to take no parameters if it isn't going to use them.
28. `Math.floor()`
29. `.push()`
30. True
31. True
32. "Tom"
33. SHIFT+ENTER
34. `popularRichGirls[2];`
35. True

Ch. 8 DIY Recommended Solution:

Here is one possible solution to the DIY Project (try typing this into the console):

```
/*
 * Candy on Halloween!
 */

// note: this doesn't have to be written inside a function!
function halloweenCandyStory() {
    let halloweenCandy = ['Kit-Kat', 'Twizzlers'];
    halloweenCandy[2] = 'Snickers';
    halloweenCandy.push('Butterfinger'); halloweenCandy.push('Almond Joy');
    halloweenCandy.unshift("M&M's");
    console.log("I think I'll eat this delicious " + halloweenCandy.pop() + '!');
    halloweenCandy[2] = 'Starburst';
    const fletchersChocolate = [
        'Milky Way',
        "Peanut M&M's",
        'Three Musketeers',
        "Hershey's"
    ];
    halloweenCandy = halloweenCandy.concat(fletchersChocolate);
    halloweenCandy.shift(); // Yum!
    halloweenCandy.sort();
    console.log('I now have ' + halloweenCandy.length + ' pieces of candy!\n'
        + 'My candy includes: ' + halloweenCandy.join(' and ') + '!');
}
halloweenCandyStory();
```

The response I got (log messages only):

```
I think I'll eat this delicious Almond Joy!
I now have 8 pieces of candy!
My candy includes: Butterfinger and Hershey's and Kit-Kat and Milky Way and Peanut M&M's and
Snickers and Starburst and Three Musketeers!
```

Chapter 9 Answers

Ch. 9 Quiz Answers:

1. Loop
2. `while`
3. `for`
4. loop / condition
5. 5
6. convention
7. Infinite! there is no incrementer, so code will be trapped in a never-ending loop!
8. `;` (semicolon)
9. Condition
10. Yes. / `Big mistake`. (the reason for this is because the `m` starts with `1` and continues until it equals the length of the array. When that happens, `top40Hits[m]` would be the same as `top40Hits[4]` which is `undefined`)
11. 18 (remember that it starts at `0`)
12. Iteration
13. `hats.length`

Ch. 9 Drills Answers:

A. Try typing these valid code snippets in the console

1. (too many lines to show here; just test this in the console)
2. `"0|7|14|21|28|35|42|49|56|63"`
3. (too many lines to show here; just test this in the console)
4. (too many lines to show here; just test this in the console)
5. `["Z", "Y", "X", ... "C", "B", "A"]` // (abbreviated)
    `"brush teeth"`
6. `A is a vowel.` // includes the other vowels too
7. (too many lines to show here; just test this in the console)
8. (type in the console. nothing to see here)
9. `0 is divisible by 10!` // includes 10, 20, 30, etc. also
10. `0 is divisible by 5!` // includes 5, 10, 15, 20, etc. also
11. `0 is divisible by 3!` // includes 6, 9, 12, 15, etc. also
12. (too many lines to show here; just test this in the console)
13. (type in the console. nothing to see here)
14. `"3 | 6 | 9 | 12 | 15 | 18 | 21 | 24 | 27 | 30"`
15. `"5 | 10 | 15 | 20 | 25 | 30 | 35 | 40 | 45 | 50"`
16. `"7 | 14 | 21 | 28 | 35 | 42 | 49 | 56 | 63 | 70"`
17. `"10 | 20 | 30 | 40 | 50 | 60 | 70 | 80 | 90 | 100"`
18. (type in the console. nothing to see here)
19. `"1 | 2 | 3 | 4 | 5 | 6 | 7 | 8 | 9 | 10`
    `2 | 4 | 6 | 8 | 10 | 12 | 14 | 16 | 18 | 20"`

20. (too many lines to show here; just test this in the console)
21. (too many lines to show here; just test this in the console)

B. What's wrong with each of these code snippets?

1. Should be `for` instead of `while`.
2. Should be `while` instead of `for`.
3. Should be `const` instead of `let`.
4. `.split()` should have a string passed in (e.g. `.split(',')`)
5. There will only be one iteration. The `return` statement causes the interpreter to immediately exit the whole function so no more looping may occur.
6. This will actually show all of the odd numbers instead of the even numbers. If the developer wants even numbers, she should've used `if (!(s % 2))` because this would resolve to `true` if the number is evenly divisible by `2`.

Ch. 9 Aggregate Review Answers:

1. comparison
2. truthy / falsy
3. False
4. Don't Repeat Yourself
5. True
6. `Math.floor(Math.random() * 40);` // note: this cannot give you exactly 40
7. Number of items in the array / number of characters in the string
8. Yes.
9. index
10. False. Block comments start with `/*` and end with `*/`.
11. `.push('new_item_goes_here');`
12. Undefined
13. Chaining
14. camelCase
15. True
16. No. You can't reassign a value to a `const` variable.
17. `floor / random / length`
18. Remainder (of an integer division problem)
19. `x` // note that it is lowercase!
20. `"phone"`
21. `"laptop"`
22. `opponentsScore++;` or `opponentsScore += 1;`
23. `%` (modulo)
24. True
25. `<` // this one was tricky. read it carefully if you got this wrong
26. False. `trainCars.length` will be 3

27. `Math.floor()`
28. Assignment--a value is being assigned to a variable (example: `let ferrets = 2;`)
29. SHIFT+ENTER
30. True
31. True
32. `var`, `let`, `const` / `const` / `var`
33. loop / condition
34. `\n`
35. convention
36. logical
37. Iteration
38. It is valid, but it probably won't do what the developer wants. It should use a `>=` sign so that it would state `"You have enough money!"` if called with the exact amount.
39. Infinite! This code would get stuck in an infinite loop because the value of `x` would continue to increase and thus the condition (`x > 0`) would always be true!
40. It is valid, but it has a bug. Nothing after the first `return` statement would get run.
41. 4 lines
42. True
43. Self-documenting
44. `!`
45. True
46. falsy / truthy

Ch. 9 DIY Recommended Solution:

Here is one possible solution to the DIY Project (try typing this into the console):

```
function amIAllergic() {
    const candyBars = [
        'Butterfinger',
        "Hershey's",
        'Kit-Kat',
        'Milky Way',
        "Peanut M&M's",
        'Snickers',
        'Starburst',
        'Three Musketeers'
    ];
    for (let i = 0; i < candyBars.length; i++) {
        const candy = candyBars[i];
        const lastLetterOfCandyBarName = candy.split('').pop();
        if (lastLetterOfCandyBarName === 's') {
            console.log("Don't eat " + candy + "! You're allergic!");
        } else {
            console.log(candy + ' is safe for you to eat!');
        }
    }
}
```

```
amIAllergic();
```

The response I got:

```
Butterfinger is safe for you to eat!
Don't eat Hershey's! You're allergic!
Kit-Kat is safe for you to eat!
Milky Way is safe for you to eat!
Don't eat Peanut M&M's! You're allergic!
Don't eat Snickers! You're allergic!
Starburst is safe for you to eat!
Don't eat Three Musketeers! You're allergic!
```

Chapter 10 Hangman Game

Here is all of my full code for the full Hangman game. Try this out in your console!

```
function generateHangmanSolution() {
    const possibleSolutions = [
        'watermelon',
        'volleyball',
        'homecoming',
        'strawberry',
        'retirement',
        'television',
        'friendship',
        'cinderella',
        'restaurant',
        'helicopter',
        'skateboard',
        'leadership',
        'antarctica'
    ];
    const randomIndex = Math.floor(Math.random() * possibleSolutions.length);


    return possibleSolutions[randomIndex].toUpperCase();
}



function gameOver(solution, won) {
    const asciiHangman = '____\n|/ |\n| @\n| /|\\\n| / \\\n|\n=====';
    let message = '';
    if (won) {
        message = 'YOU WIN!';
    } else {
        message = 'GAME OVER\n\n' + asciiHangman;
    }
    message += '\n\nThe correct answer was ' + solution + '!';
    alert(message);
    return message;
}
```

```
/************************************
 * Main Function for Playing Hangman! *
 ************************************/
function playHangman() {
    const solution = generateHangmanSolution();
    const solutionLetters = solution.split('');
    const wrongGuesses = [];
    const maxWrongGuesses = 7;
    const progressSoFar = '_'.repeat(solution.length).split('');


    const confirmPlay = confirm("Let's play Hangman!\n\n"
        + "Pick letters to guess the word I'm thinking of.\n"
        + "It's a common word with " + solution.length + ' letters.\n'
        + 'Are you ready to play?');
    if (!confirmPlay) {
        return gameOver(solution, false);
    }


    while (wrongGuesses.length < maxWrongGuesses) {
        const promptMessage = 'Here is your progress on the word so far: \n'
            + progressSoFar.join(' ') + '\n'
            + 'Wrong Guesses: [' + wrongGuesses.toString() + ']\n\n'
            + 'Pick a letter!';
        const userInput = prompt(promptMessage);


        if (!userInput) {
            return gameOver(solution);
        }


        const guess = userInput.toUpperCase();
        let goodGuess = false;


        for (let i = 0; i < solutionLetters.length; i++) {
            if (solutionLetters[i] === guess) {
                goodGuess = true;
                progressSoFar[i] = guess;
            }
        }


        if (goodGuess) {
            if (progressSoFar.join('') === solution) {
                return gameOver(solution, true);
            }


            alert('Good guess!');
        } else {
            wrongGuesses.push(guess);
            alert('Sorry, ' + guess + ' is incorrect.\nYou have '
                + (maxWrongGuesses - wrongGuesses.length) + ' strikes left.');
        }
    }
```

```
    return gameOver(solution, false); // if player gets here, Game Over (fail)
}


playHangman();
playHangman();
playHangman();
```

Glossary of Terms

(**technical term** *[chapter in which it was introduced]* - definition.)

- **acronym** *[ch. 2]* - shortened words that are usually made from taking the starting letters of other words...like LOL (laugh out loud) or BTW (by the way).

- **argument** *[ch. 4]* - value passed into a function to be assigned to the function's parameters. When a function is called and values are "passed in" (by putting those values in the parens while invoking the function), these "passed-in" values are called arguments.

- **array** *[ch. 8]* - a list of values in a specific order. An array is used to store multiple values in a single variable.

- **assignment** *[ch. 1]* - JavaScript statement involving a variable on the left side, and a value on the right side. The variable takes on the value that is assigned to it.

- **augmented assignment** *[ch. 2]* - A shorthand way of writing both an operation and an assignment. It first performs an operation on the variable and then *assigns* the new value to that same variable. Examples: `+=`, `-=`, `*=`, and `/=`.

- **block comment** *[ch. 3]* - may span multiple lines; causes the interpreter to ignore everything from the `/*` until it finds `*/`.

- **bold** *[ch. 1]* - thicker darker text.

- **boolean** *[ch. 5]* - One of the 5 primitive data types. Rhymes with "truly inn." The value of a boolean is always either true or false.

- **break return** *[ch. 3]* - technical term for a new line in coding.

- **bugs** *[ch. 1]* - mistakes or unintended results in code.

- **built-in** *[ch. 4]* - provided by the JavaScript language itself (not custom made by the developer or a third-party library).

- **camelCase** *[ch. 1]* - a readable form for writing function and variable names—starting with a lowercase letter and containing a capital letter at the start of each word (or acronym). It's called camelCase because the capital letters in the middle of the word kinda look like the hump(s) on a camel's back.

- **chaining** *[ch. 8]* - repeatedly calling one method after another on an object, in one continuous line of code.

- **character** *[ch. 3]* - individual single piece of a string (a single letter, digit, or symbol).

- **Chrome** *[ch. 1]* - the internet browser of choice for working through this book.

- **code** *[ch. 1]* - [When used as a noun:] instructions that a computer reads and follows to produce a program or display a page. [When used as a verb:] to write instructions for the computer to follow.

- **comment** *[ch. 3]* - single-line or block comments; the interpreter ignores these lines in the code. Used for human-readable statements or to temporarily hide lines of code from the interpreter if you don't want them run.

- **comparison operator** *[ch. 5]* - symbol used for comparing two values; always results in a boolean value. Example comparison operators: ===, !==, <, <=, >, and >=.

- **computer** *[ch. 1]* - the physical thing that you do your work on--either a desktop, laptop, or Chromebook (for the purposes of this book, NOT a smartphone or tablet!)

- **concatenate** *[ch. 3]* - combine two or more strings (or numbers with strings) to create one longer string.

- **condition** *[ch. 5 & 9]* - (when referring to a comparison operator) results in a boolean value and determines if the code is executed; (when referring to a loop) the thing that let's you know to keep repeating the block of code that's being looped. Once the condition is not met (no longer truthy), it's time to stop repeating the looped code.

- **conditional** *[ch. 5]* - A conditional statement in coding is used to perform certain blocks of code based on a given condition. The condition (for example, a comparison operator like x === y) results in a boolean value (true or false). If the boolean value results in true, the code is executed (run). Otherwise, the code block is skipped (doesn't run).

- **console** *[ch. 1]* - part of Chrome's top-secret developer tools. Used for testing out bits of JavaScript and even interacting with the webpage you're on.

- **constant** *[ch. 7]* - an unchangeable value.

- **convention** *[ch. 9]* - A guideline that recommends a specific programming style, decision,

215

or standard—not because it's required but because it is a common, accepted practice in the industry. Example: camelCase.

- **custom** *[ch. 4]* - created yourself (not *built-in* the language itself or created by a third-party library).

- **data type** *[ch. 2]* - What *kind* of value a variable represents. There are 5 data types covered in this book: number, string, boolean, null, and undefined.

- **debugging** *[ch. 1]* - walking through your code looking for errors ("bugs") in order to fix them (squash them).

- **declare** *[ch. 1]* - define (introduce) a brand new named variable or function into your code. This only happens once per variable or function.

- **decrement operator** *[ch. 2]* - a shortcut for taking a number and *subtracting* the number 1 from it (sometimes known as "decrementing"). Example: `myNumber--;`.

- **define** *[ch. 1]* - a value is given to a variable or function name. Afterward, that variable or function name can be used to represent that value.

- **developer** *[ch. 1]* - person who writes code (a.k.a. programmer or engineer).

- **DIY** *[ch. 1]* - "Do It Yourself" project. You can do this on your own, then compare your code to my solution in the Answers section.

- **documentation** *[ch. 7]* - written-out explanations for what code does or how to use it.

- **DRY** *[ch. 4]* - "Don't Repeat Yourself". Principle in coding where you try to define things only once and reuse functions, variables, code blocks, and class libraries instead of retyping the same code again and again.

- **e.g.** *[ch. 2]* - short for "example."

- **engineer** *[ch. 1]* - person who has a full-time job as a developer (a.k.a. programmer).

- **error message** *[ch. 1]* - response from the console that tells you what is wrong with your code. This is your friend.

- **escape** *[ch. 3]* - to use a backslash (\) before a character that might normally have specific instructional meaning in code (such as a quote mark or apostrophe) to make the interpreter read it just like part of the string. Example of escaping an apostrophe: `let wordWithApostrophe = 'can\'t';`

- **Euclidian division** *[ch. 2]* - fancy name for integer division (see glossary definition).

- **evaluate** *[ch. 4]* - to process something like a function or a variable. When the JavaScript interpreter invokes (runs) a function to get its return value, it can be said to be *evaluating* that function.

- **falsy** *[ch. 5]* - Not actually a boolean data type, but treated the same as a boolean `false` for purposes of conditional statements such as `if...else` blocks. E.g., empty string (`""`).

- **function** *[ch. 4]* - a separated block of code that can be called to perform a specific task.

- **glossary** *[ch. 1]* - it's like a dictionary that only has terms from this book.

- **i.e.** *[ch. 1]* - short for "in other words."

- **increment operator** *[ch. 2]* - a shortcut for taking a number and *adding* the number 1 to it (sometimes known as "incrementing"). Example: `myNumber++;`.

- **index** *[ch. 8]* - when working with arrays, it's the number representing any given item's position in that array (beginning with 0). So the first item in an array has an index of `0`, the second item has an index of `1`, etc.

- **internet browser** *[ch. 1]* - a program that you use to go to websites. Chrome is the one we use for this book. Other internet browsers are Firefox, Safari, Edge, or Internet Explorer (IE).

- **integer division** *[ch. 2]* - (a.k.a. "Euclidian division") division that ignores all fractions (rounding down) and ignores the remainder (or separates out the remainder to be returned from modulo operation).

- **interpreter** *[ch. 1]* - inner program that reads and executes (runs) your code.

- **invoke** *[ch. 4]* - a fancy name for calling a function (actually running the function by typing its function name followed immediately by parens).

- **iteration** *[ch. 9]* - a single pass through of a looped code block.

- **JavaScript** *[ch. 1]* - front-end programming language used in all browsers (and the only programming language used in this book).

- **log** *[ch. 4]* - write down info somewhere (often displayed in the console window).

- **logical AND** *[ch. 6]* - logical operator that determines if the values on *both* sides of `&&` are truthy. If left side is truthy, it returns the value for the right side. If left side is falsy, it returns the left side value (ignoring the right side). E.g., `(5 > 2) && 12;` returns `12`.

- **logical NOT** *[ch. 6]* - logical operator that returns a boolean (`true` or `false`). It will return `true` if placed before a falsy value and `false` if placed before a truthy value. Example: `!true;` returns `false` and `!(3 > 5);` returns `true`.

- **logical operator** *[ch. 6]* - evaluates an expression to test if it is truthy or falsy. May result in non-boolean values. Example logical operators: `&&`, `||`, and `!`.

- **logical OR** *[ch. 6]* - logical operator that determines if the value on *either* side of `||` is truthy. If the left side is truthy, it returns the value for the left side (ignoring the right side). If left side is falsy, it returns the right side value. E.g., `5 || (1 === 0);` returns `5`.

- **loop** *[ch. 9]* - a block of code that will repeat itself over and over again until some condition is met.

- **method** *[ch. 7]* - a function belonging to an object or class. Any property of an object that points to a function is called a method.

- **modulo** *[ch. 2]* - (or mod or modding) operator—represented by a `%` sign—used to get the modulus (remainder) of an integer division problem. Example: `5 % 3 === 2;`

- **modulus** *[ch. 2]* - remainder of an integer division problem.

- **negative** *[ch. 2]* - less than zero.

- **nested** *[ch. 4]* - one function inside of another function, or `for` loop inside of another `for` loop, or HTML element inside another HTML element, etc.)

- **null** *[ch. 6]* - one of the 5 primitive data types in JavaScript—it basically means *nothing*. It also resolves falsy.

- **number** *[ch. 2]* - one of the JavaScript data types. Pretty much any number you can think of (even infinity). May be positive, negative or zero and may or may not have a decimal in it. Never shown with quotes.

- **object** *[ch. 7]* - a collection of properties (name/value pairs).

- **operating system** *[ch. 1]* - The software that runs all of the programs on your computer. If you're using a PC, your operating system is Windows. If you're using a Mac, it's MacOS. If you're using a Chromebook, it's ChromeOS.

- **operator** *[ch. 2]* - (`+`, `-`, `*`, `/`, and `%`) used for adding, subtracting, multiplying, dividing, and modding numbers as well as concatenating strings.

- **parameter** *[ch. 4]* - variable within the parens in a function's definition. When the function is called, different values--called arguments--are passed in and assigned to each of the temporary variables of that function (called "parameters").

- **paren** *[ch. 1]* - short form of the word "parenthesis" (and "parens" is short for two or more "parentheses"). Examples: `(` and `)`.

- **positive** *[ch. 2]* - greater than zero.

- **primitive** *[ch. 5]* - data type that is not an object and has no methods (functions) in itself.

- **programmer** *[ch. 1]* - person who writes code.

- **programming language** *[ch. 1]* - set of words and symbols that the computer understands and interprets in a certain way when reading a program. Examples are: JavaScript, Python, Java, PHP, and many more.

- **property** *[ch. 7]* - a named value that is attached to an object.

- **self-documenting** *[ch. 7]* - when the names of variables and functions explain well what your code does. This makes it easier to read and understand, without the need for many comments or lengthy documentation explaining things.

- **separator** *[ch. 8]* - when converting an array to a string, this is the small string that is placed in between each item of the array.

- **single-line comment** *[ch. 3]* - causes the interpreter to ignore everything from the `//` to the end of the line.

- **statement** *[ch. 1]* - a single piece (usually one line) of instruction in JavaScript code.

- **string** *[ch. 1]* - one of the 5 primitive data types in JavaScript—made up of individual characters and usually shown with quotes.

- **syntax** *[ch. 1]* - it's like the spelling and grammar of the programming language—the form and order that the computer expects to see the code.

- **troubleshooting** *[ch. 10]* - looking for the cause of a problem and fixing it.

- **truthy** *[ch. 5]* - Not actually a boolean data type, but treated in the same way as the boolean `true` for purposes of conditional statements such as `if...else` blocks. Example: any non-zero integer.

- **undefined** *[ch. 6]* - one of the 5 primitive data types in JavaScript. It's the default value of a variable and implies that no other value has been assigned. It also resolves falsy.

- **variable** *[ch. 1]* - a named location that can store different values in a JavaScript program. It can often be changed.

- **Workbook** *[ch. 1]* - the name I use to refer to the document (usually in Google docs) that you use to type out all your answers to quizzes, drills, and DIY projects.

ABOUT THE AUTHOR

Jeremy Moritz has been developing software since 2004 and currently works as a senior software engineer in the Midwest. Along with computers, Jeremy has coached chess and has an extensive background as a musical theater director, choreographer, and performer, having been involved in the production of over 100 musicals with children and adults of all ages. As a longtime teacher and homeschooling father of six children, Jeremy has valuable insight into common learning habits and hang-ups of children and teenagers. With his background as a performer, he exhibits a flare for comedic writing that is sharp and entertaining. Jeremy and Christine—his illustrator and devoted wife of 16 years—live with their children in Kansas City, Kansas. Feel free to contact him at www.CodeForTeens.com!

ABOUT THE ILLUSTRATOR

Christine Moritz has been drawing since she could hold a crayon and is a lifelong lover of all things creative. When she's not doodling, she can be found expressing her creativity through her love of piano, cooking, and power tools. *Code for Teens* is the first book she has ever illustrated, but it is one of many collaborative projects she has undertaken with her husband, Jeremy.